onestepahead

Organizing and Participating in Meetings

Judith Leigh

Cartoons by Beatrice Baumgartner-Cohen

OXFORD

UNIVERSITY PRESS

For my colleagues past and present, especially Beth, Chris, Laraine,
Doug, Anne-Marie, Guy, Faye, and Richard

OXFORD UNIVERSITY PRESS

Great Clarendon Street, Oxford OX2 6DP

Oxford University Press is a department of the University of Oxford.
It furthers the University's objective of excellence in research, scholarship,
and education by publishing worldwide in
Oxford New York
Auckland Bangkok Buenos Aires Cape Town Chennai
Dar es Salaam Delhi Hong Kong Istanbul Karachi Kolkata
Kuala Lumpur Madrid Melbourne Mexico City Mumbai Nairobi
São Paulo Shanghai Singapore Taipei Tokyo Toronto
with an associated company in Berlin

Oxford is a registered trade mark of Oxford University Press
in the UK and in certain other countries

© A. J. Leigh 2002

The moral rights of the author have been asserted
Database right Oxford University Press (maker)

First published 2002

British Library Cataloguing in Publication Data
Data available

Library of Congress Cataloging in Publication Data
Data available

ISBN 0-19-866284-X

10 9 8 7 6 5 4 3 2 1

Design and typesetting by David Seabourne
Printed in Spain by Bookprint S.L., Barcelona

Organizing and Participating in Meetings

Judith Leigh is a history graduate from the University of London. She has held a variety of administrative posts in commercial and non-commercial companies.

THE LEARNING CENTRE
HAMMERSMITH AND WEST
LONDON COLLEGE
GLIDDON ROAD
LONDON W14 9BL

One Step Ahead

The *One Step Ahead* series is for all those who want and need to communicate more effectively in a range of real-life situations. Each title provides up-to-date practical guidance, tips, and the language tools to enhance your writing and speaking.

Series Editor: John Seely

Titles in the series

Editing and Revising Text	Jo Billingham
Essays and Dissertations	Chris Mounsey
Organizing and Participating in Meetings	Judith Leigh
Publicity, Newsletters, and Press Releases	Alison Baverstock
Punctuation	Robert Allen
Spelling	Robert Allen
Words	John Seely
Writing for the Internet	Jane Dorner
Writing Reports	John Seely

Symbols used in this book:

know your target audience

technology/ computer issues

Contents

1 Groundwork

*Every time you
say 'hello' you
start a meeting.*

Introduction

Meetings are part of life. Every time we say 'hello' we start a meeting of some sort. A lesson at school, an evening out with friends, buying things at a shop: all these are types of meeting. As your career progresses or if you decide to take an active part in local affairs, you will find yourself involved in more and more meetings. But the word 'meeting' can be very daunting if you are not used to attending formal meetings and everything which they involve. Knowing how to organize or participate in a meeting is a key skill and experience that can help you, whether it is a work situation or in private life.

This initial chapter is divided into four sections:

- a brief note to show you how to use this book to gain the most from it whatever your role is in a meeting;

- an introduction to the concept of meetings—what they are for and how they reach their aim;

- the jargon often used at meetings;

- the titles and roles of participants.

Together, these form the groundwork for both participating in and organizing a meeting.

Using this book

This book is intended to take you through all the stages of a meeting, from setting one up to putting the decisions made at a meeting into practice.

Part A takes you through each step of a meeting, while Part B provides flowcharts, checklists, and templates for quick reference. In Part A, cross-references to other chapters or items in Part B are given in the margin.

Also in the margins are a variety of quotations about meetings. Some may make you smile, but it's worth thinking about whether they are appropriate to your meeting, or to the way you approach attending a meeting. If you find sympathy with too many of the negative views, perhaps it's time to work out a new strategy.

Each chapter begins with a short introduction to the topic it covers and states who the chapter is mainly aimed at: the organizer of the meeting, the participants, or the Chair of the meeting (who may not be the same person as the organizer). However, you will probably still find it useful to skim through the chapters which don't affect you personally now. In the future you may be the organizer or the Chair, even if you are a plain participant at the moment. In addition, you may find tips about organizing or chairing that you can pass on to the people responsible for these aspects which will help the meeting as a whole.

Excuse me, I'm looking for the Loch Ness Monster meeting

What is a meeting?

Essentially, all meetings are to review and discuss what has happened, decide what to do next and agree how to do this. Meetings usually therefore have a circular structure:

Meetings have a circular structure.

Meetings may have only one or two of these elements. A 'brainstorming' meeting will be concerned with deciding what to do next and how to do it. A sub-committee set up to discuss a particular issue may consist of reviewing a situation, determining what to do next and reporting back to the main meeting. When a meeting is first set up, it is important to decide which of these elements the meeting is responsible for, and also to ensure that all the participants know what the limit of the meeting's responsibility is. Without this clear direction, the meeting and its participants may issue instructions without actually having that power. This leads to confusion about decision-making and can make an organization take actions it did not intend to!

On pages 110–13 in Part B there is a list of meetings and what their usual purpose is.

Meetings go by all sorts of names—management meetings, sub-committees, steering groups, board meetings, council meetings, departmental meetings, appraisals.

Even though meetings may go by the same name, every meeting differs from another because the people participating in it are different. This means there is no single key to holding a successful meeting; but there are standard factors—such as good preparation and obtaining a mix of people who work well together—which will make a meeting constructive.

The language of meetings

There are some words widely used and accepted in meetings which are not exactly jargon but which you may not have come across before, or which have a slightly different meaning in meetings compared with normal life.

Agenda: The agenda is the list of topics that are to be considered at a meeting.

See Chapter 3 for more on agendas.

Agreement, proposal and resolution: These terms all imply a form of assent to a suggestion. An agreement is a simple statement of fact, for example, 'It was agreed that the budget would be discussed at the next meeting.'

A proposal usually arises out of a discussion, for example, 'After discussion, John Smith proposed that the Chair should write to the local MP.'

A resolution has a legal implication and has a formal status. Resolutions are made when a decision is taken to change the way an organization is run, for example, 'It was resolved that the Chair should serve for a term of five years.' Banks and other institutions may also require that organizations take resolutions when making financial decision, such as setting up a direct debit facility.

> **Tip**
> Each meeting has its own language which grows up with it, and these are only common examples. You might want to start making your own list of words and phrases so that you can refer back to them.

Chair: The Chair of a meeting is the person who runs the meeting when it is in progress. To chair a meeting is to be in charge of the meeting.

See Chapter 5 for more on being the Chair of a meeting.

Consensus: A consensus is a majority view by the participants of the meeting, for example, 'There was a consensus that the budget should be discussed next.'

Minutes: Minutes are the record of what happened at a meeting. *A minute* is the record of one event at a meeting. *To minute* a meeting is to take notes of the discussion. *To agree the minutes* is to accept that the minutes of a previous meeting are accurate.

See Chapter 6 for more on minutes.

Motion: A motion is a suggestion to take some form of action. The phrases 'table a motion' or 'a motion on the table' are used when a participant raises a suggestion at a meeting.

See Chapter 3 for more on papers and reports.

Paper: A paper is the written explanation which accompanies an item on the agenda. This may take the form of a report on a project or business activity, the financial accounts for a given time period, or a draft resolution.

Quorum: In formal meeting situations, a quorum is the number of people who must be present for the meeting and its decisions to be legal. A meeting is 'quorate' when the relevant number of participants are present.

Tip
Do you know what the quorum is of your meeting? Check the Memorandum and Articles of Association, or other governing rules. If there is none at the moment, should there be one to make the meeting always representative of the views it covers?

Speaking 'through the Chair' or 'with the Chair's permission': These are terms used at formal meetings. Participants use them when they want to ask a question of another participant, and observers should ask to speak 'with the Chair's permission' when making a point.

Table: In the UK, papers are tabled when they are passed around to participants at a meeting. In the USA, to table a matter is to set it aside for an indefinite period. If you are in an international meeting, make sure that the participants are clear which meaning is being used. (See also 'Motion' above.)

Although the modern trend is to avoid jargon, Latin phrases are often used in formal meetings. The list on page 115 in Part B gives a short list of ones you might encounter.

Voting

A *show of hands* is the simplest way of voting, when participants raise their hands to agree or disagree. If you are holding a large meeting, for example an AGM, appoint tellers to count the number of hands in a specific section of the room. Alternatively, use voting papers which participants hand in after each proposal: this takes time, but is an accurate method of counting and is confidential. Participants who cannot attend the meeting may be entitled to a *proxy vote* by which they formally appoint a member who is at the meeting to vote on their behalf. *Postal votes* may also be used, where participants complete a ballot paper before the meeting. These votes are then added to the number of votes at the actual meeting.

Who's who in meetings

Participants in meetings have a variety of titles. These titles may be just 'courtesy' titles and have no implication other than denoting seniority, but some names have definite responsibilities and legal meanings. Where the titles fall into this second category, it is important to use them to ensure that decisions taken at the meeting are fully endorsed in legal terms.

Note that, with the exception of the Chair, not every meeting has or needs each of the following participants. Where possible, and especially in informal meetings, try to avoid handing out titles which can smack of bureaucracy.

Chair, Chairman, Chairwoman, Chairperson: the Chair of a meeting is responsible for managing the meeting in accordance with the rules of the organization. Chair is the most commonly used title.

Vice-Chair: The Vice-Chair is the Chair's deputy, and is responsible for running the meeting if the Chair is absent. In some circumstances, the Chair will decide to step down from the chair during a meeting, so that he or she can speak more freely. In these circumstances, the Vice-Chair temporarily takes over the running of the meeting.

Company Secretary: In a public limited company and other organizations which are governed by company or charity laws, the Company Secretary has legal obligations to run the organization in accordance with this legislation. It is the Secretary's responsibility to make sure the meeting is held according to these laws and in accordance with the governing rules—usually known as the Memorandum and Articles of Association—of the organization. The Company Secretary often combines this role with that of Chief Executive, or is also the accountant responsible for the financial affairs of the company. It is usually the Company Secretary's job to put into practice any decisions made by the meeting or to decide who will implement the actions needed. The Secretary will also complete and file any legally required papers with, for example, Companies House, and assist in the preparation of a company's Annual Report.

Tip
To encourage people to take part in meetings, try to give everyone a role at the meeting. This does not mean giving everyone a title, but do give each person a job. These roles could include minute taking, vote counting, keeping the meeting to time, presenting a report, leading questions on a report.

More on the role of a Chair in Chapter 5.

A public limited company or PLC is one where the liability of the shareholders is limited either by a fixed number of shares or by a guarantee incorporated in the rules of the company. Companies trading on the Stock Exchange must have PLC status.

Committee Secretary: The Committee Secretary looks after the paperwork associated with a meeting. The Secretary might also be responsible for booking the venue, taking minutes, and generally organizing the 'nuts and bolts' of a meeting.

Minutes Secretary: The Minutes Secretary is responsible for taking the minutes at meetings, writing them up afterwards and circulating them to participants. The Minutes Secretary might also perform the duties of the Committee Secretary, but generally their work begins and ends solely with the minutes.

President: A President may be a well-known public or trade figure appointed as a 'figurehead', who is the public face of the organization. In this case, the President is unlikely to have many powers at a meeting, though as a courtesy they may be invited to the meeting and asked to chair it. Alternatively, it may be a title denoting the senior manager in a business organization (especially those with an American management structure) who has the same powers as a Chair. Vice-Presidents in similar organizations will be the heads of departments or strategic areas. They will be expected to report at senior management meetings on this area and hold their own meetings to determine the state of play.

Treasurer: The title 'Treasurer' is given to the person responsible for financial matters in non-commercial organizations such as charities and trades unions. The Treasurer will make recommendations to the meeting about the accounts and budgets. Some organizations, especially schools and other educational establishments, may call this role 'Bursar', although the Bursar may also be responsible for administrative matters.

Ordinary participants at meetings may be known by a variety of terms, for example:

■ *members*—often used for trade or other organizations with a membership element. The participants represent the rest of the members;

Who's the boss?

Meetings must be quite clear who has the final say on what the meeting is to discuss or on any decision made. This responsibility generally belongs to the Chair, but confusion can arise if the President of an organization attends a meeting but is not the Chair. Be clear from the outset of the meeting who's in charge.

- *delegates*—frequently used at conferences, where participants are invited to give news of progress or to give opinions;

- *directors*—in most use in commercial organizations, where participants have a stake in the business;

- *shareholders*—for commercial companies with a share capital;

- *governors*—best known in educational or institutional arenas;

- *committee members*—a general term for anyone attending a specific type of meeting;

- *attendees*—implies participants who have a passive role, so should be avoided.

Of these terms, 'director' has a legal significance, as directors can be held accountable for actions taken by their organization.

You may also come across the word 'observer' to describe someone who attends a meeting. Observers cannot actively participate in decision-making, but make recommendations to the meeting as a whole. They are asked on the basis of their experience or expertise. Legally qualified advisers, financial advisers, and senior managers from the organization often fall into this category.

Sherlock Holmes famously observes to Dr Watson in 'A Scandal in Bohemia': 'You see but do not observe.' Observers have a vital role to play in meetings, spotting issues that may not be obvious to other participants.

In some cases, participants may combine several titles in their role. For example, a Director may also act as a Minutes Secretary, or the Treasurer may also be the Vice-President. If you are in this position, it is important to make sure that you have enough time for the demands of the role—and that there is no conflict of interests between the roles.

Participants may combine several titles in their role.

2

Why, who, where, and when

Introduction

Successful meetings are the result of careful preparation. Although it can seem time-consuming, taking pains over setting up a meeting reaps its own rewards. The resulting meeting is constructive, with all participants knowing what the meeting is about, who will be there, where to go, and what to discuss. They leave knowing what they need to do next. Crucially, they will also want to come back for the next meeting.

The cornerstones of this preparation stage are the four 'W's:

■ *Why* is the meeting being held?

■ *Who* should be there?

■ *Where* should the meeting be held?

■ *When* should the meeting take place?

This chapter looks at the four 'W's, together with suggestions for making them as easy as possible. This chapter will be of most use to organizers or Chairs of meetings; but if you are a participant, you may also find it helpful to read through to find tips to pass on to the organizer of your meeting.

Why?

Decide what you want the meeting to achieve.

It sounds very obvious to say that you must decide why your meeting needs to happen, but it is surprising how often the purpose of a meeting is not clear, especially if it is the first time the meeting has been held. If there is no defined reason for the meeting, it can turn into a talking shop, with little agreed and participants leaving dissatisfied and demotivated. Therefore, the first thing you need to do is decide broadly what you want the meeting to achieve. Write these aims down so that you can refer to it when you come to the later 'W's, as this list affects how you decide to deal with them. This list is a little different from an agenda, which contains topics you will discuss to achieve the broad aims.

Your list of aims should be quite short: perhaps even one line. Try not to have more than four aims; more will mean the meeting has so many things to discuss it will turn into a summit conference.

2 Why, who, where, and when

Agendas are discussed more fully in Chapter 3.

 Do!

keep to a simple list of aims.

 Don't!

expect your meeting to achieve more than half its aims in the first year of existence.

Examples of aims

Scenario 1: You are setting up a local action group to campaign about a proposed plan to build on open fields.

Aims:

○ see who can give time to the campaign, and who will just support you;

○ organize a method of campaigning;

○ decide how to raise money for the campaign.

Scenario 2: You are taking over the management of the Residents' Association of your block of flats.

Aims:

○ continue the usual management work of the Association;

○ get more residents involved in the Association.

Scenario 3: You have been asked to set up a sub-committee of the Staff Council to discuss a specific issue.

Aims:

○ discuss the issue;

○ make a report of the recommendations.

Who?

Once you have decided why you are holding the meeting, you need to decide who to ask to achieve your meeting aims. If you are taking over a meeting as in Scenario 3 above, the participants will already be decided; in Scenario 2, the members of a sub-committee are generally appointed by the main meeting body.

However, if you are setting up a meeting for the first time, as in Scenario 1, you need to think about the range of skills and experience you require in your meeting to achieve your broad terms. The typical skills you need in a new meeting are:

- people prepared both to talk *and* listen—people who only talk are not good news in a meeting!

- people ready and able to give time up for the meeting—people may be very interested in the meeting, but if they can only give you every third Tuesday between half past three and four o'clock they already have too many calls on their time and will not be able to give enough attention to your aims;

- people genuinely interested in the issue—those who are only interested in the social status conferred on them by being asked to join a meeting are unlikely to contribute constructively or usefully to the meeting. Boasting about their importance is not helpful to the way your group will be viewed by others.

Don't fall into the trap described by the person who said: 'A committee is a group of the unwilling, chosen from the unfit, to do the unnecessary.'

 Do!

look for a balanced mix of people.

 Don't!

appoint people who always agree with each other.

If you are arranging a meeting about local affairs, beware of only asking friends to participate. Meetings made up only of friends run the risk of being considered biased and exclusive by outsiders. Aim to have a half-and-half mix of friends balanced with others who may be 'nodding acquaintances' or complete strangers to you. If the meetings go well, you will have gained new friends!

In management textbooks, you will often find lists of types of people such as coordinator, shaper, implementer, plant, team worker to describe how people behave in a team or working environment. Just as successful teams are supposed to contain one person of each type, you need to try and put together a group of participants with different characteristics so that everyone brings some different ability to the meeting. Here are four types of people you should aim to include to hold a productive meeting:

- *coordinator*: a person who leads the meeting, steers the discussion, and keeps a grasp of everything that needs to be taken into account in the discussion, such as staff and finances. Often the Chair of the meeting;

- *doer*: a person who will carry out the decisions of the meeting. Doers often find meetings frustrating as they prefer to do rather than talk, but their presence is essential because (a) they will carry out the decisions of the meeting and (b) they will understand from the discussion at the meeting why they are carrying out the actions involved in a decision;

- *contributor*: a person who will speak at meetings but may not do much outside the meeting. These people are useful, as they often bring an outside eye and balanced view to discussions;

- *researcher*: a person who will check facts and figures of any suggestions made at a meeting. Researchers usually have a strong grasp of the subject under discussion and are important as they often spot the weak point in an argument.

2 Why, who, where, and when

Do!

check your list of potential participants against your list of aims: who will constructively help you achieve them?

Don't!

approach the same people over and again to be participants. Firstly, such people's time is already taken up with other issues; secondly, you will be recirculating the same ideas. Look for new blood and new ideas.

No grand idea was ever born in a conference, but a lot of foolish ideas have died there.

(F Scott Fitzgerald, *The Crack Up*)

Be brave enough to hold brainstorming meetings where all sorts of ideas can be discussed. Realizing what won't work is just as important as identifying what will.

BRAINSTORMING MEETINGS

Although participants need to work together as a team, it is important to mix people with different views in some types of meetings, especially brainstorming meetings. Participants who always agree are unlikely to produce the groundbreaking ideas that come from such sessions. A handful of people with off-the-wall ideas and opinions can make all the difference between a company being—often dangerously—complacent and opening up new avenues for progress. These sessions are a challenge to the Chair; but they have to be challenging to achieve their aims.

Tip
When you start asking possible participants to a meeting, check at what dates and times they will be available. There is more about this on page 20.

You also need to consider the experience and knowledge that people will need both to be interested in the meeting and to participate actively in the meeting. Some standard experience and skills are:

■ *previous experience in a similar field:* participants will be able to draw on their own experience and make recommendations from this, so avoiding past mistakes and capitalizing on past successes;

■ *financial/accounting qualifications or work experience:* essential if any sort of accounts are to be presented at the meeting or financial matters are to be discussed;

■ *legal qualification or experience:* in more formal meetings, legal knowledge is useful for drafting resolutions or contracts. If the meeting is a management meeting of an organization with a constitution, a legally qualified participant can check that the meeting is run in accordance with the constitution.

Once you have identified your list of potential participants, taking into account their personal circumstances, characteristics, and experience, you will need to invite them to the meeting.

When you are first setting up an informal or local affairs meeting, the best approach to possible participants is a telephone call, explaining the purpose of the meeting and asking if they would be interested in attending. Follow up the call with a letter confirming the date and time of the meeting. When you do not know the person, you can ask someone who does know them to make the initial phone call to sound them out. If the reply is favourable, you should then call to explain in more detail what the meeting is about. Again, follow up your call with a confirming letter.

Where you are arranging a more formal meeting, start by writing the person a letter explaining who you are and why you are writing, and saying you will call them on a given day to talk the meeting over with them, for example:

The Johnson Trust
c/o 42 Smith Street
Birmingham B1

Dr J Ryan
The Surgery
67 Jones Drive
Birmingham B15

27th September 2001

Dear Dr Ryan

Re: <u>New Standing Committee</u>

The Johnson Trust proposes to set up a standing committee to discuss long-term care for patients at home. The Chair of the Committee will be the Professor of Geriatric Medicine from the university. I have been asked to act as Committee Secretary.

The Chair and I would like to invite you to be part of this standing committee, as we would value your opinions and advice based on your experience of working with local patients.

The first meeting will be held in October at the Johnson Trust offices. I enclose the proposed agenda. I will call you on Thursday to discuss the meeting in more detail, but if you would prefer to call me before then, my number is 0999 123456.

Yours sincerely

Jane Smith

In the example to the left, reference is made to a Trust. If you include names of people or organizations in your opening letter, make sure that your reader knows who or what these are and if not, include an explanation. If you have a company or charity brochure, attach this to the letter.

Note that you should also give the participant the option of calling you.

Remember that some people will not want to attend your meeting. Don't take the refusal personally: people have other calls on their time or may not want to be actively involved. Respect their decision but leave the door open for them to change their mind. If you organize a 'good' meeting, the word will get round that your meeting is worth attending.

When?

Before starting to determine the date of your meeting, decide who will contact participants. The Committee Secretary is the usual person to carry this out, but the job may be carried out by the Chair in non-work situations. Whoever it is, ensure that only one person does the work, to save time for both organizer and participant.

Do!

leave enough time to make calls: nothing is more offputting than someone trying to rush a participant into agreeing a date.

Don't!

forget to reintroduce yourself to the participant if you are following up an introductory letter.

Finding a date and time when a number of people are all free can be difficult. If your meeting is small (up to four people) a few phone calls will be enough to arrange a time, but to help yourself, start with a couple of dates in mind. Where you have more than four people involved, you might find it useful to make a table as on page 119 of Part B. As you make your calls you can fill in the availability of people in your table.

You will frequently find that people are unable to give you a definite yes or no for a given date. Put these dates in as 'difficult' in your plan and try to avoid them.

Being unable to contact a participant often happens, and in such a case you have to make a decision. (Obviously if the participant is the Chair of the meeting, you can decide nothing until you do make contact.) Alternatively, ask the Chair what they want to do. The Chair may tell you to go ahead and arrange the meeting or wait for the person's availability. In the latter case, put contacting the participant at the head of your list of priorities each day. When time begins to run out, you will need to contact the Chair again and ask them for a decision. If the Chair decides to cancel or postpone the meeting, contact the other participants to tell them what is happening and why.

If you are meeting on a regular basis, try fixing the dates of all subsequent meetings at the first meeting of the year, or your initial meeting. All the people needed to fix dates will be in one place, which saves phoning around, and participants will immediately know the dates meetings will be held on. Circulate a confirming list after the meeting. Remember, however, if any changes to the dates are made later, to send round a revised list to everyone, drawing their attention to the change.

Finding a date can be difficult.

If you are the Chair of the meeting, your decision whether to go ahead with booking a meeting when one participant's date preferences are not known rests on the importance of the person to the meeting. Although everyone who's invited to a meeting is important, you will know if the meeting will be a waste of time without the person or can proceed, perhaps with the cancellation of one discussion item. You could also ask the person unable to attend to send in a short written report instead.

> Henry Ford, the American car manufacturer, held his management meetings at 5.10pm on Fridays. His theory was that his managers would be so keen to leave at 5.30pm for the weekend that they would concentrate on the matter in hand and not get sidetracked into lengthy explanations. Just to emphasize his point, he had no chairs or table at the meeting, as he had noticed that people were quicker at making decisions standing up.

What else?

The other point you need to take into consideration when fixing a date is whether anything else needs to happen before your meeting, or if an action needs to be taken directly after it is held. For example, if you are organizing a branch trade union meeting, you might need to attend the central committee meeting beforehand, to inform your branch of the decisions taken there. Alternatively, the central committee might be waiting for your decisions, so you must ensure your meeting takes place before the central committee's meeting.

What else needs to happen before you hold your meeting?

Where?

Where you decide to hold your meeting is determined by four factors: the type of meeting, the size of meeting, the money available to pay for a venue and the location of the various participants.

Settings for different meetings

Match your venue to your meeting.

The mood of a meeting can be influenced by the place in which it is held. It is important that you match the meeting to the setting so as not to confuse participants with mixed messages. For example, if you hold a formal meeting in a wine bar, your participants will probably not be able to hear properly over the noise—and their main focus could be on the wine list. On the other hand, a brainstorming session held in a boardroom can overwhelm the participants into formality when the atmosphere needs to be relaxed.

- An **informal** meeting should be held in an informal setting. This could be anywhere from your lounge to having the meeting over a meal at a local restaurant.

- A **formal** meeting demands a formal environment. In a work situation, book a meeting room. School governors' meetings can be held in a room within the school. Local venues such as village halls and function and conference rooms within hotels can also be used.

External venues will ask if you want your meeting 'boardroom' or 'conference' style. See the plans on page 123 of Part B for what these terms mean.

- A **public** meeting such as an AGM calls for a substantial venue. This does not need to mean pompous. Museums, art galleries and other public attractions (such as zoos) can often cater for events in a unusual setting, which provide a talking point for people attending the function. If you are looking for a more restrained atmosphere, local institutions and clubs generally have rooms available, and their boardrooms can be very impressive.

> When calling an external venue, ask for the Conference, Events, or Banqueting Manager, who will have all the facts ready to hand.

Size of venue matches size of meeting

You obviously need to find a venue large enough to seat everyone at the meeting comfortably. If possible, you should visit your chosen venue. Brochures that claim a room 'seats 20' can mean 'seats 20 if everyone sits two inches apart'. Ideally, there should be enough space for participants to leave the room without more than one or two people needing to move their chairs or stand up. If there are refreshments being served such as tea and coffee, there should be enough room for the server to circulate round the table with ease.

Some meetings may not require a table at all. If your meeting consists only of presentations you could arrange the chairs in a row with a small table at the front for the presenter to put down his or her notes. In a discussion-only meeting, putting chairs in a ring can help give an open feeling to the session.

For an all-day meeting, you might also see if there is enough space at the venue for there to be a 'breakout' area, so that during intervals in the meeting people can move away from the meeting room altogether to stretch their legs and get a change of scenery. Hotels are perfect for this type of meeting, as there is usually a lounge or bar area for people to go to. If you are serving a meal during the meeting, this should certainly be laid in a separate room, otherwise the post-meal session of the meeting can end up being held in a room smelling strongly of food.

Tip
If you are arranging an AGM where you do not know how many people will attend, check the records to see how many people previously attended and add on 10% to allow for new members arriving. For a public meeting, arrange enough space to accommodate around 30% of your target audience. Some venues have rooms with removable partitions, so that if the worst happens and many more people than expected arrive, the room can be expanded.

Look for external funding.

See Chapter 9 for ways to get round having to have face-to-face meetings.

Tip
Once you decide where and when to hold your meeting, send out a confirming letter to all participants, giving details of
- date
- time
- venue (with a map if appropriate)
- transport arrangements
- overnight facilities
- any equipment participants need to bring.

Funds available

Your choice of venue may be limited by your financial resources. If money is tight, shop around and negotiate a price with an external venue. You may be able to negotiate a discount if your meeting is held regularly and you can give the venue a list of confirmed dates: venues are always keen to secure a guaranteed income source.

You could also try checking with funding organizations such as the local Council or charities if your meeting is eligible for a grant. Local sponsorship may also help, but the payoff may be having to invite the sponsor, so be careful to check there is no clash of interests!

Location of venue and participants

You need to choose a venue whose location is reasonably central to all the participants. Extensive travelling time can put off potentially useful participants. If you are planning a meeting for an organization which pays travel expenses, arranging a meeting at a distant location can prove very expensive.

There are exceptions to this rule. One example is if you are arranging a training meeting. This should take place away from the usual environment to minimize interruptions to the trainees. If the training is being carried out by an organization, it will generally be able to offer dedicated training facilities.

As you develop your organizing skills, you may be asked to arrange a conference which takes place over several days. In this case, you should look at hotels offering conference facilities, as you will also need to arrange accommodation for the delegates. What type of hotel you choose depends again on the type of meeting and your budget. The more prestigious the event, the more prestigious your venue. Country house hotels offer a setting which concentrates delegates' minds on the meeting, while town hotels offer a range of attractions outside the meeting venue: this latter is useful if you are expected to arrange an evening programme of entertainment or events for partners accompanying delegates.

You may also need to organize transport for participants at a meeting. This could include:

Local parking arrangements. Book spaces in the company car park if available or confirm where the nearest public car park is and send directions to participants. You may also find it useful to have a supply of small change for parking meters.

Local public transport. Participants often find the journey between the mainline rail or coach stations, or the airport the most difficult part. Check timetables and inform participants which bus number or train destination they require.

Flights. Confirm which airline, the flight numbers and times of arrival and departure. Always remember to book a return flight unless specifically asked not to. You might also want to book a taxi from the airport to the meeting venue to help your participant have a stress-free journey. If you are really organized, you could also check for delays on the day of departure.

> All travel tickets should be delivered to participants by either courier or registered post.

Some other points to consider when booking a venue

- Is there anyone with a mobility impairment or other additional physical requirement? Check disabled access at the venue. Some meeting rooms are also fitted with an induction loop for the hard of hearing.

- Is there anyone with special dietary requirements? Remember to check their menu requirements if you are providing refreshments at the meeting. If you have vegetarians or vegans attending the meeting, remember to include a dish for them in the menu, which should be clearly marked 'vegetarian/vegan'.

- Check with the venue on possible restrictions on use. While most venues are non-smoking now, there may be other restrictions such as a ban on red wine (because of potential damage to fixtures and furnishings), out-of-hours access, or photography.

■ If there are to be presentations at the meeting, check that overhead projectors are available, or a screen for computer presentations—plus a handy socket for plugging in the computer. If you have time before the meeting, check the equipment to ensure a smooth run-through in the meeting.

■ Check the small print for hidden charges. Venues usually charge for overhead projectors, videos, and television screens, but flipcharts should be free.

More help

■ If you are organizing an international conference, you may also need to arrange translation services, both oral and written. Local translation services are listed in the telephone directory or national services on the Internet, while venues may also have recommendations. When you set up your room, remember to reserve space for the translators.

■ Take along a small box of 'emergency' items to a distant venue. Suggested items are a spare bulb for the overhead projector, a disc holding any computer presentations, spare company literature, and business cards. Programme numbers of essential contacts into your mobile phone—but don't forget to turn it off during the meeting.

Agendas, papers, reports 3

Introduction

Although meetings are all about talking, the paperwork behind the meeting is just as important. In this chapter, we look at three types of paperwork that all meetings need.

This chapter is for everyone involved in a meeting. As an organizer you will find out what paperwork is needed and how to manage its presentation; as a Chair you will see what your organizer should be doing on the paperwork front; as a participant you will learn how to write paperwork for a meeting and how to read papers sent to you. As organizer or participant you will learn ways to keep track of all papers through a filing system.

Agendas

The agenda for a meeting is a list of the individual items that need to be discussed to reach the meeting's broad aims.

Agendas may be drawn up and circulated to all participants before the meeting, or they may be agreed at the actual meeting. The first method is generally preferred for formal meetings, where agenda items are often accompanied by a written explanation. It is important to decide who is responsible for drawing up the agenda (usually the Chair in conjunction with the Company Secretary or Chief Executive).

The second method suits informal meetings, where participants are invited to bring suggested topics for discussion with them to the meeting. Remember, however, that meetings are not infinite; participants will need to agree which topics are most important, so that the meeting does not run on forever.

The agenda is the list of individual items that ensure that the meeting achieves its broad aims.

Tip
Make sure
participants know
how to request an
item be included on
an agenda. A letter
to all participants
inviting them to
propose agenda
items a week or so
before the agenda
and accompanying
papers are drawn
up is one way to
achieve this.

Participants may also ask at a meeting for topics to be considered at the next meeting. The Chair or Committee Secretary needs to keep a note of these for inclusion in the next agenda, and to coordinate any reports from staff or participants which need to accompany such topics.

Common agenda items

Some agenda items, as the topics on the list are called, are used in almost every meeting. The following explains the most common and gives the order in which they should appear.

■ **Apologies for absence**: Every meeting should start with a note of participants who are unable to attend. As a matter of courtesy, participants should notify the Chair or organizer that they are not attending.

■ **Minutes of the last meeting:** A review of the minutes of the last meeting so that everyone agrees that these are correct or agrees on any amendments. In formal meetings, the Chair will sign the agreed minutes at this point.

■ **Actions since last meeting (or Matters Arising):** It is a good idea to pick up on decisions and actions that were made at the last meeting to see what has happened since then.

Specific items

see pages 116–18 of Part B for more about financial terms.

The meeting should now consider the topics that are specific to its own business. These might include:

■ **Finance/Accounts/Budgets:** This item should always be accompanied by a set of the latest accounts with a report drawing participants' attention to particular matters of importance in them.

■ **Appointments:** A report on vacancies and appointments, both within the meeting and, if appropriate, on the staff. Vacancies or appointments about to happen should also be included so that participants are kept fully up to date.

- **Special Reports:** These could include reports on progress made on a project at a previous meeting (for example, the installation of new computer equipment), proposals for new projects (for example, a suggestion to upgrade computer equipment), reports on problems encountered by the organization and proposals for their resolution (for example, the lack of computer equipment, its effect on the business of the organization, what equipment is needed, what it would cost, and how funds can be found).

Concluding items

The final two items on an agenda should be:

- **Date of next meeting:** Even if the date is already set, it can be helpful to remind participants when and where the next meeting will be held. Participants also then have the chance to say if they will not be at the next meeting, and this can be noted.

- **Any other business (often known as AOB):** This is the chance for participants to raise minor matters not included on the main agenda, such as thanks to a departing member of staff. To raise an AOB matter, participants should request permission from the Chair to speak. Participants should not raise important matters under Any Other Business, such as financial or constitutional matters. The rule of thumb is that items raised under Any Other Business should not require an explanatory paper.

Other common agenda items

In formal meetings, the meeting may be required formally to **adopt the agenda** at the outset of the meeting—meaning that the participants accept that these are the topics they want to discuss. If a participant wants to discuss additional subjects, the rest of the participants must decide whether this is appropriate. Again, the simple rule is that if it is a topic that needs a written explanation for the meeting to consider all the implications before it is discussed, then the subject should not be added.

Agendas and time

Plan your agenda to fit the time allowed for the meeting. You can specify on the agenda how long each item will be discussed for (e.g. ten minutes, twenty minutes). Time planning depends to a certain extent on experience: if you are new to this area, ask seasoned participants how long standard items generally take. Try also to leave a spare ten minutes to allow for unexpected discussion, additional items raised at the meeting, and the late arrival of participants.

The Law of Triviality

Briefly stated, it means that the time spent on any item of the agenda will be in inverse proportion to the sum involved.

(from *Parkinson's Law* by C. Northcote Parkinson)

Pages 124–5 in Part B show a template agenda.

The meeting may also need to **appoint a Chair** or other officers. If this is the case, this needs to be the second item after the Apologies for Absence.

There may be **resolutions** for the meeting to agree. These should be listed as separate items, for example:

> Resolution to implement a direct debit facility

or

Tip
Underlining the wording in a resolution helps pinpoint the proposed change for participants.

> Resolution to propose to the Annual General Meeting that Article 14 of the Association be changed to 'the Company Board shall consist of <u>fifteen</u> directors, as voted for by the shareholders in accordance with Article 12.'

The order for agenda items

Adoption of Agenda
Apologies for
    Absence
Appointment of
    Chair (or other
    officers)
Matters Arising
Financial/Accounts/
    Budget
Appointments
Special Reports
Resolutions
Date of Next
    Meeting
Any Other Business

When drawing up an agenda, check that, where items are connected (so that if one proposal must be agreed before the next is made or a report must be given to make sense of a proposed action), you put them in the right chronological order on the agenda.

For example, if you want your meeting to agree to set up a direct debit facility for the organization, put the report on why you need this facility before the resolution. The agenda would read:

Item 2: Report on bank charges for cheques

Item 3: Resolution to implement a direct debit facility

Annual General Meeting agendas

Tip
AGM agendas often have to be sent out to participants within a specified time frame—usually at least two weeks in advance of the meeting. Check your Articles of Association or other governing rules for the right dates.

AGM agendas have a set pattern of items, according to the nature of the organization and company law. The agenda must clearly state the date, time, and place of the meeting. The usual items on the agenda are:

- *Apologies for absence*: The names of anyone entitled to be at the AGM but who has informed the organization they cannot attend should be read out. However, if this list runs into hundreds, the list of names can instead be posted up somewhere in the room where the AGM takes place. Very large organizations may dispense with this item altogether.

■ *Minutes of the last meeting*: The minutes should be circulated with the AGM agenda.

■ *Adoption of company report and accounts for the last financial year*: The company report and the audited accounts should be included with the agenda.

■ *Appointment of auditors for the company*: The name and address of the proposed auditors should form part of this agenda item, for example:

To appoint Smith & Sons of 42 Great Street, Melchester as the auditors of the Company

■ *Appointment of new directors*: Following resignations or at the end of a fixed period of office, there will need to be a vote to fill the vacancies. Names of proposed new directors should be included on the agenda.

■ *Resolutions regarding changes to the Memorandum and Articles of Association*: A report explaining the reasons for the change should accompany the agenda, together with the wording of the Memorandum and Articles as they stand.

■ *Any other business*.

Tip
The end of the agenda should have the words 'By Order of the Company Secretary', be signed by the Company Secretary, and have the Secretary's name underneath the signature.

Papers and reports

The papers and reports that accompany the agenda can make or mar a meeting. Well-written and presented papers which clearly put the case for a recommendation or report on a situation are more likely to find favour with participants. If you are the participant, you will gain better knowledge of the subject under discussion from a 'good' report.

Well-written papers will find favour with participants.

In meeting terms, a **paper** usually contains a proposal, while a **report** is an update on a situation.

As the art of report and paper writing is a big subject, this section only gives some pointers. If you want to improve your skill in this area, you will probably find it useful to read books dedicated to this topic.

See the section on Further reading and resources at the end of Part B, page 137.

Your paper or report needs to follow a logical structure. Start with a short statement of what it is about. This immediately focuses the reader's mind on the subject. Suppose you are suggesting buying new swings for a school playground. In this first section you would write:

> This paper is a proposal to purchase new swings for the school playground.

You then need to write the reasons why you are making this proposal: a review of the present situation.

> The swings that are currently in the playground are beginning to show signs of metal fatigue and some parents have expressed concerns about their safety.

You should then go into your proposal in more detail, explaining how it could be carried out, the timescale, and any financial costs involved in that action. Try to give at least two ways of carrying out the action so that the meeting can see you have thought your proposal through and are aware that there are alternatives which you have decided are not suitable.

> It is therefore proposed that we should take down the existing swings and replace them with four new swings. The work will take approximately a week, and to keep disruption to a minimum it is suggested that this should be carried out during half-term.

> The cost of new swings will be £1,000 and the work to take down the existing swings and replace them has been estimated by John Jones Builders at £500. The Parent Teachers Association has generously agreed to fund the new swings. John Jones Builders has agreed to reduce their bill by £250, if we book this work in with them by the end of the month.

> The alternative is not to replace the swings; but as we all know, these are one of the most popular items in the playground.

This format works well for formal papers to a formal meeting, but a shorter and punchier approach would be more appropriate for presenting a proposal to colleagues in a work situation. In this case, using a memo either in hard copy form or by email is a simple alternative. For example, suppose you are part of an informal 'staff entertainments committee' and are responsible

Tip

Three simple rules for report and paper writing are:

1. Keep it short.

2. Keep it simple.

3. Avoid jargon.

If your paper or report includes technical terms specific to the topic which you are writing about and which participants may not have come across previously, either explain the word the first time you use it in the report or include a glossary at the end of your report. This also applies to abbreviations and acronyms for equipment and organizations. For example, if you are a computer expert, the terms WAN and LAN may be obvious to you, but your reader needs to know not only what these acronyms stand for (wide area networks and local area networks) but also what they are.

for suggesting venues for the staff Christmas party. Your memo might run as follows:

MEMO
FROM: Claire
TO: Amanda, Ed, John, Susan
DATE: 5th October 2001

RE: CHRISTMAS LUNCH & PARTY

I have now visited three venues which are suitable for the Christmas lunch:

1.Café Blue: good traditional menu, space a bit limited (£15 a head)

2.Jo's Wine Bar: modern menu, good atmosphere (£20 a head)

3.Magnolia House: traditional and modern menu, own room which can be changed over for disco later on (£30 a head).

I suggest we go to Magnolia House. We went to Café Blue last year so it would be good to have a change. Jo's modern menu may not appeal to some staff.

I need to let Magnolia House know by the end of the week: please let me know your thoughts at tomorrow's meeting.

The above examples are fairly straightforward proposals. Where you have more complex matters, for example the purchase of a new building, your paper will be much longer, as there are many more options to consider. If your report runs to more than two sides of A4 paper, you should consider putting in a header page with a summary of the report.

Do!
include a summary where your report is longer than two sides of A4 paper.

Don't!
forget to include timescale and costings in your summary.

Summary

■ proposal to purchase area adjoining the playground on west side of school;

■ current situation: lack of space for pupils for sports activities;

■ cost implications: £15,000 purchase price; £5,000 to prepare the area for use;

■ raising the money: suggestions for fundraising to augment budget for such purposes;

■ timescale: decision required in the next two weeks.

The above are examples of papers. In a **report**, you should structure your writing round the individual tasks undertaken in the project. Take time to identify these tasks and their logical order, so that the report is easy to follow.

Returning to the playground swings example, suppose you now want to write a report on their installation. The title would be:

Erection of the new swings in the playground

Again, this focuses your readers' minds on the subject and makes it clear from the start what your report is about. If you are half-way through a project, you might want to add the date to the title, to show that this is what has happened up to the date of writing the report, and that the project is not yet finished.

Erection of the new swings in the playground: Progress Report 13th January 2001

Split your report up into the various activities involved in the project. In the case of the school swings these would be:

- purchase of new swings;
- demolition of old swings;
- installation of new swings;
- donation of new slide;
- addition of plaque;
- accounting.

Under each section, give a brief résumé of what has happened, any problems encountered, and how they were tackled. State what work remains to be done and the timescale in which the work will be done. For example:

Demolition of old swings

Demolition began on the first day of half-term. We had hoped that this would be completed during half term to minimize disruption to normal school life. Unfortunately, due to the very severe weather, work overran by two days into the term, but we are pleased to report that the builders have now finished.

Include anything that has cropped up during the course of the project which was not discussed at the original meeting.

Donation of new slide

Mrs Harrison, retiring headmistress, has generously donated a new slide to the playground. This was installed at the same time as the swings without further cost to the project. Mr Evans, Health & Safety officer, checked and approved the slide.

Tip
If you are in charge of a project, be very careful about agreeing to extra work without gaining permission and agreement from the meeting.

As a project progresses you may need to return to the meeting to put forward a further proposal. Extra proposals can be included in your report, but use **bold** print or <u>underlining</u> so that readers can see at a glance their importance.

Addition of Plaque

The PTA has suggested that a plaque be attached to the slide, recording Mrs Harrison's gift. **It is therefore suggested that a plaque be purchased for £50 with the wording, 'Donated by Mrs Harrison, Headmistress of Finching School 1987–2001'.**

Reports for an informal meeting, like papers, need to be shorter. After the staff Christmas party has taken place (see page 33), you might want to confirm what was a success and what wasn't, for future reference. A memo as follows would be a solution:

MEMO
FROM: Claire
TO: Amanda, Ed, John, Susan
DATE: 6th January 2002
RE: CHRISTMAS LUNCH & PARTY

Just a note to confirm the feedback I have had from the party.

- Everyone liked the venue.
- The food was disappointing. Several of the menu options were cancelled at the last minute.
- Staff have asked if this year's party could be held earlier as several employees had already left for their Christmas holidays.

Otherwise, it was one of the best parties we have held! Special thanks to Amanda for her hard work on this.

Sections and numbering

In longer papers and reports, it is important that your readers can find their way quickly around the text and, in meetings, pinpoint the section they want to talk about.

All papers and reports should be page numbered as a starting point in this process. Page numbering also helps to ensure that participants receive the right number of pages. Each separate paper and report can be numbered individually, or each 'pack' accompanying an agenda can be numbered sequentially, with the agenda as page 1. If you are coordinating a number of papers and reports, tell the writers which page number they should use as their first page.

Tip
Be careful with numbering systems. Put in too many sub-sections, and you will end up with something along the lines of the following.

1.3.iv.7.6: proposal for fundraising (continued): proceeds of bring and buy sale

This smacks of red tape and is confusing to the reader.

Sections should be titled, and you may also want to number them. In this way, if you have a secondary point you want to make within the main section, you can keep it separate within the main text. For example:

> 5: Appointment of New Head Teacher

> 5.1: Salary and benefits

Your readers then know that the whole section is about the appointment of the new head teacher, and there is a 'special' subject included in this section about the teacher's salary and benefits.

If you refer in your paper or report to another section of the same paper or report, put the page or section number in the reference so that your readers can find it easily. For example:

 Do!
use an appendix to take complicated details out of the main text.

> The costings outlined in Section 2 (page 6) show that the department can afford to recruit two new assistants.

 Don't!
forget to state in the text that more information is included in the appendix.

Appendices

In a formal paper or report with a lot of detailed information, it can be useful to put this information in appendices, rather than in the main text. This means your readers are not bombarded with data, and the flow of your argument is not inter-rupted. If, for example, you are on the management committee of a block of flats, and are proposing to carry out extensive repairs to the building, you could include the tenders from con-tractors as appendices, while giving a brief breakdown of the important facts in the actual paper.

Once you have completed your paper, it is useful to put in the top right-hand corner the agenda item which it accompanies, to avoid any confusion on the reader's part.

Finishing your paper

When you have finished writing your paper or report, read it through. If you have time, put it aside after writing it and read it through a day later. You will notice more errors or confusions in the text if you give yourself a break from it. Pay particular attention to spelling: if you are using a word-processor, spell-checking programs do not always spot correctly spelt but incorrectly used words, for example:

right write	now know	were where	affect effect
of off	too two	heard herd	ensure insure

Spell-checking programs also usually use American spelling which may not be acceptable in your meeting. Check with the Chair or Committee Secretary what form of spelling is standard for papers and reports.

Learn from the editing of papers and reports.

You may need to submit your paper to the Chair or another senior member of the meeting before it is sent out with the agenda. In this case, be prepared for some editing to be done. Don't take editing personally—it is intended to clarify any questions and tidy up style. Learn from the editing so that you will produce better papers and reports in the future. You should, however, ask to see the edited copy before it is sent out, in case a proposal or report does not tally with your views. In this case you will need to discuss with the editor why such radi-cal changes have been made. Don't jump to conclusions, but hear what the editor has to say.

Reading papers and reports

Reading maketh a full man; conference a ready man; and writing an exact man.

(Francis Bacon, *Of Studies*)

When you are reading papers, have a pen and paper to hand so that you can make notes or jot down queries as you read. By the end of the paper you should know what the current situation is, what is being proposed and why. You should also see if there are any cost implications and how those costs are to be met. For reports, check for anything not originally agreed and for missed deadlines. You should also check for things that have gone well: praising people at meetings is very popular with the people who are carrying out the project.

If anything in the paper is unclear, you have the choice of bringing this up at the meeting or contacting the writer of the paper before the meeting to ask them to explain the point. What you decide to do depends on the nature of your query. The following are guidelines to use:

- If you don't understand any of the paper or report: talk to the writer.

- If you don't understand the proposal: wait until the meeting.

- If you don't understand one or two terms: talk to the writer.

Some people view it as an embarrassment to say that they don't understand a paper or report, but being confident enough to say you don't understand is a key skill of being a participant. Without participants willing to say this, meetings can easily become 'rubber-stamping factories', where all proposals are agreed without question. For any organization, this is potentially disastrous, as actions may be taken which have serious implications for the survival of the organization.

...and this bit about hyperinflationary pressures countering demographic transition just means the office move is off?

If you don't understand ... talk to the writer.

However, you should approach your reading of papers and reports with an open mind and consider proposed changes. Finding this balance between caution and optimism is the aptitude which marks out those meetings which are seen as dynamic but which do not lose sight of the practical details.

Sending out the paperwork

How

When you send out the agenda, papers, reports, and any other paperwork for a meeting, it can make a pile that is daunting to the recipients. You need to find a way to encourage participants to read the papers, and to give them a method by which they can keep track of paperwork. Trying to find stray pieces of paper an hour or two before a meeting can be very frustrating.

One way to start your sending-out procedure is to put together a 'master pack' containing a copy of the agenda and all accompanying papers. Check and recheck the master pack, asking yourself

■ Are all the papers there?

■ Are all the papers in the right order?

■ Are all the papers legible?

If your papers and reports have page numbers, the easiest way to check that each pack is complete is to flip through the pages spotting any gaps in the numbering.

To reproduce your master pack, either photocopy or, if all the documents are on one word-processor, print off the right number of copies. Bear in mind that photocopying (if you have ready access to a photocopier) is cheaper than printing copies. If you are on a tight budget, ask participants who are preparing papers to send you the right number of copies.

The last question in the list above refers to the quality of the photocopying: it's a false economy to send out badly photocopied papers as no-one will read them. You also need to check that all the pages have been photocopied. Photocopiers are

 Do!

assemble all your papers in one master pack and check them through against the agenda before photocopying or printing the rest of the participants' packs.

 Don't!

assume that a photocopier always copies every page: check that each pack contains all the papers.

Tip
Always make a few extra copies of your master pack, and take these along to the meeting in case participants arrive without their pack.

notorious for taking two originals through their system in one go and hence missing copying a page.

Once you have all your packs prepared, choose one of the following methods for sending them out:

■ ringbinder;

■ slide-on binder;

■ wire or heat binding.

A piece of coloured paper inserted between the individual sections can also be helpful for recipients.

If posting your packs, use a strong envelope which will cope with the weight and the wear and tear received in the post. Again, participants are less likely to read papers that arrive dog-eared and torn through the post. If your packs are very large, you may also want to contact your recipient to warn them a parcel is on the way. If participants are out at work or elsewhere, they may need to make special arrangements for receipt of an item that will not go through the letterbox.

If you are sending a bulk mailing of papers, for example, for an AGM, check with the Royal Mail or other carriers for discounts and special collections direct from your office or home. The Royal Mail's website address which gives details of the various services they can offer is www.royalmail.co.uk.

You may want to use a mailing house when you have a mailing running into thousands. The mailing house will ask you to supply labels, or label information on a computer disk from which it can print out the labels. You generally need to pay the postage costs in advance to the mailing house: work out the rough cost by weighing a typical pack for the correct postage, then multiplying this by the number of items to be sent out. If your mailing includes overseas addresses, add more to your cheque to cover this.

Using email

With the growth of email facilities, one way to cut the costs of sending out papers right down is to send all the papers out as attachments to an email. Offer participants the opportunity to receive the documents electronically and point out the cost saving.

If you do choose this method to send out papers, load the attachments in the order they should be read. It is also sensible to ask participants to email back to you that they have received the papers. If you receive no reply from a participant after two days, follow up with a phone call—the participant's email may not be working.

Beware of sending multiple or very long attachments to emails, as some computers cannot cope with downloading many megabytes of information. This is particularly the case if the attachments contain many graphics.

As a matter of courtesy, take the trouble to check that any documents you send by email are free of viruses, especially those which have been sent to you for forwarding to participants. If you suspect that you have inadvertently sent on a virus and cannot contact one or more of the participants by phone, send another email with the subject box completed as 'URGENT: do not open previous email, contains virus.'

When to send out papers

For most meetings, aim to post or email papers at least a week in advance of the meeting and preferably a fortnight before. This gives participants time to read through all the papers and follow up any queries they may have.

Formal meetings, such as AGMs, may have the timing of receipt of papers laid down in the organization's constitution, so you will need to check this carefully.

If you have new participants joining a meeting, send them a pack containing the agenda, accompanying papers, and minutes of the last four meetings. This will enable them to get a feel for what the meeting does and how it is run, together with background knowledge of the issues under discussion.

Do!

leave enough time in your schedule for the unexpected.

Don't!

forget to book in time for printing with internal or external printers.

When you are dealing with a mass mailing the whole process can take up to six weeks, so timing is of vital importance. In this case, it can be useful to work your timetable backwards. If you know that the papers must be with the recipients by a certain date, you know what date the papers must be posted. Therefore, all the papers must be ready by x date. Talk to your printers to check they can meet the date and what their deadline is for printing. You can then tell the writers of the papers what date you must receive their work ready to go to the printers. You may also need to factor a mailing house into your timetable: they will take a day or two to package up the papers. Allowing up to a week for things to go wrong is a good safety net. The following is an example of a timetable:

Date of AGM: 1st November

Date papers must be received by (2 weeks prior): 18th October

Date of posting (allow 4 days): 14th October

Date of delivery to mailing house for packing (2–3 days): 11th October

Date for delivery to printers (1 week): 4th October

Date for final checking by Chair (1 week): 27th September

Date for delivery of papers for first check (1 week): 20th September

Keeping track of your paperwork

Find a method for keeping track of paperwork.

As a recipient of meetings papers, you should set up a filing system to ensure that you can find any paper you want from any meeting. A lever arch file with dividers or a document wallet will help you divide up the papers. You can choose whether to file them according to subject matter or according to the meeting for which they were produced. The first method can be time-consuming, but you do not then have to remember which meeting a particular topic was discussed at to find the paper in the future. Alternatively, if you file the papers by meeting date, you could make an index of papers by subject matter to help you locate them in the future. You will probably also find it useful to have a box file for bulky papers that cannot be easily hole-punched.

If you are the organizer of the meeting, you should keep copies of all the papers and file them for future reference. In this case, it is best to have them filed according to meeting date, but again, you are advised to create a subject index of papers.

3 Agendas, papers, reports

An example of a subject index is given on page 126 in Part B.

Minutes of meetings of organizations with a constitution (including schools and charities) must by law keep a copy of all signed minutes ready for inspection by both members and any regulatory bodies. Strictly speaking, these should be kept in a locked cabinet, accessible only to authorized persons. A deed box or filing cabinet is fine for this purpose.

Electronic storage

If you receive papers by email, you may wish to store them on your computer rather than taking up space with paper. However, it is important to arrange your electronic files just as logically as paper-based files. Putting documents in a single folder is a starting point, but you could also divide the documents into further sub-folders arranged by year or subject.

Consider using an Intranet or Extranet on which to store meeting documents where participants can read and download as required.

Computer programs also frequently have an indexing facility where sections of each document can be logged and found by key words. Within individual documents you can also conduct word searches to find past proposals on reports or remarks by specific participants.

Many organizations now have an Intranet which can be viewed by staff and which stores internal documents. The extension to this is an Extranet, whereby people from outside log on to this facility through a password and view documents. Extranets and Intranets are an ideal way for storing meeting documents for reference by participants, but security measures for confidential documents must be well thought through and penalties imposed for not adhering to them.

Tip
Remember to keep a backup of electronic documents on floppy disk.

4 Debating and discussing: taking part in a meeting

Remember that to talk effectively, you must know your subject: start by reading the paperwork!

Introduction

At the beginning of the last chapter, we said that meetings are all about talking. This chapter looks more closely at ways of talking at meetings so that you participate actively, effectively and constructively. This chapter is therefore for everyone who takes an active role at a meeting.

When you talk at a meeting, you will do so for different reasons. These reasons are:

- presenting;

- getting information;

- discussing;

- proposing;

- disagreeing.

It is these five areas which this chapter concentrates on.

A note of warning in advance, though. The American writer Laurence C. Coughlin has the excellent suggestion: 'Don't talk unless you can improve the silence.' Many meetings are spoilt by participants believing that they *must* say something and make their presence felt. This belief counteracts the progression of the meeting, and is often a reason for participants being bored and the meeting itself being viewed as achieving nothing productive. If you keep to the five reasons above for contributing to a meeting, then the meeting will remain constructive and be well regarded.

Presenting

Usually, the first thing that will happen at a meeting is that a participant will **present** a topic. The participant may want to make out a case for an intended course of action, or bring other meeting participants up to date with progress on a project. The paperwork accompanying the meeting will—should—include a paper or report on the topic, but most meetings also like to hear from the person who has written that paper or report. Some meetings will expect a full presentation, with a display of charts and diagrams, when the project is complicated or brand new.

For a short presentation on a simple matter, you need to summarize your paper in two or three sentences. In just the same way as you structure your paper, structure your speech:

Meetings are about talking ...

■ Remind your audience of the current situation.

■ Explain the suggestion that's being made to change the situation.

■ Say why this suggestion is the best solution.

Suppose you are a member of the local Residents' Association and have put forward a paper suggesting that you meet on Thursday evenings rather than Sunday afternoons. At the meeting you might say:

> We've had a lot of difficulty finding people who can regularly attend Sunday afternoon meetings. [the current situation]

> I'm therefore proposing that we change our regular monthly meeting to the evening of every first Thursday. [the suggestion]

> I've chatted to most of you and it seems that Thursday evenings are much easier for people to keep clear. [reason why the suggestion is the best solution]

Once you have finished your presentation, the Chair of the meeting will invite questions and suggestions from the rest of the participants. See the section on 'Being questioned' on page 51 for tips on dealing with this stage of the meeting.

If you are making a more complex, radical or wide-reaching proposal you will need to make a longer presentation. In such cases the paper you have written and circulated with the agenda is the backup to the presentation you will give at the meeting. Your presentation will still follow the same structure as above, but you will need to go into more detail on the situation. There may, for example, be a range of ways of changing the situation which will need discussion by the rest of the meeting.

Take again the Residents' Association example, but this time suppose you want to suggest that the people on the management committee of the Association should be more representative of the residents. You might start by saying:

As you are all aware, we have had a number of complaints about the management committee recently. [the current situation] One point that has been raised several times is that there are very few recent or new residents on the committee [expanding the current situation] and this means that they find it difficult for their concerns to be heard. [still expanding the current situation]

In the paper I sent out to you, on page 5, I've shown the lengths of time the current committee members have served. [adding detail to the current situation]

We could consider permanently allocating one of those places to a new resident who's been here less than a year but more than 3 months [the first suggestion] or we could introduce a system whereby management committee members serve no more than 2 years at a time, to make sure there is a fair rotation on the committee of all residents. [the second suggestion]

On page 7 of my report you will find descriptions of three methods we could use to change the way we select our members to make sure we are representative of all the residents. [the third suggestion with details]

Because there are three solutions offered to the current situation, in this case you leave the debate open at the end, but you might conclude by urging your fellow committee members to consider this matter very seriously, as the committee is losing credibility with the residents.

A presenter may invite meeting participants to interject as he or she speaks. However, make sure if you do decide to raise a query during the presentation that it is at the appropriate time. Don't, for example, start asking about costs when the presenter is still talking about aims! Wait until the appropriate moment, and if it does not appear, wait until the end.

Using projectors and computers in a presentation

When you are engaged in a long presentation you may find it useful to use an overhead projector to note down the points you particularly want your audience to consider. These may be pre-prepared or you may jot them down in the course of your talk. You can also use the projector to note down comments made by the other participants. In the example below, the wording for a suggested resolution has been put up on the screen:

The Committee resolved to appoint Johnson & Brothers as their solicitors.

Using technology in your presentation can give impact to your case and drive home the message to your audience.

After discussion, the Committee has decided that some amendments to the original wording need to be made. You can now write on screen

The Committee resolved to appoint Johnson & Brothers as their solicitors for a period of one year from 1st September 2001 on an annual retainer of £5,000.

More sophisticated presentation aids such as videos and dedicated presentational software (such as Microsoft's PowerPoint) can also be used. Use of these aids can be impressive and help to drive home your message, but you need to make careful preparation in advance to ensure that your presentation is seamless and professional. Bear the following pointers in mind:

 Do!

check all the equipment works before the meeting.

 Don't!

forget to have paper backups of a presentation to hand out afterwards.

- Check that the hardware you use works properly: too many meetings are held up while faulty wiring or temperamental computers are sorted out. Try to have a rehearsal beforehand to check everything is in working order.

- When you have a rehearsal, time yourself: one slide roughly equals one minute of speech.

- Avoid having lots of text on a slide: keep to three or four bullet points or one key sentence to drive a message home.

- Cartoon animations can be fun and inject humour and life into your presentation, but don't leave these up on the screen. Show them quickly, then move on to a blank screen or the next slide, otherwise your audience's attention will be distracted from what you are saying.

Getting information

The reverse side of presenting is listening and drawing out from the presenter all the relevant information. This is a very important skill, as it enables you to make balanced decisions.

We spoke of the importance of reading all the paperwork in advance of the meeting and making notes about anything that you don't understand. Have your list of queries to hand as you listen to the presentation at the meeting, and see if any of those queries have now been answered. Tick off those which have been answered, those which need more detail, and those not answered at all.

To gain your information, you ask questions. You may have heard of the terms **open** and **closed** questions.

Closed questions are questions which demand a straightforward yes or no in reply, or a short statement of fact as their reply, for example:

Judge a man by his questions rather than by his answers

(Voltaire, quoted in *Quotations for our Time*, edited by Laurence Peter)

When will the building of the new school hall start?

or

Will the building be finished on schedule?

Closed questions usually start with the words *when, where, who.* Use closed questions when you want to establish a fact. When you want to get an opinion, or more details about a given issue, use an **open** question. Open questions often start with the words *how, please tell me, give me your opinion, what do you think?* For example:

What do you think the effects of the builders' strike will be on the building of the school hall?

or

How do you see the new Chairman working with the new regulations?

You will probably need to use a mixture of closed and open questions to gain the information you require. You can start with a closed question to establish a fact, following this up with an open question which will ascertain the replier's opinion on that fact.

What you should try to avoid is asking multiple questions in one go, as the person you are asking will find this confusing. Instead, warn your replier that you have quite a few things to ask and take the questions one step at a time. The following is an example of how *not* to raise a question:

> Could you give some more details about this scheme to build the new school hall, for instance how long you think it will take to build and whether the funds we have are available and if not, how we should raise the funds?

The role of the Chair during a question session is crucial. The Chair must keep questioners to the point and be strict about allowing only one person at a time to raise a question.

The person replying will have got lost half-way through this. The only question they are likely to answer is the last one about raising funds, as the last part is the part people remember. Try also to be definite when asking a question. In the example above, asking for details about the scheme to build the new school hall was vague. 'Some more details' doesn't actually mean anything. *What* details do you want and what depth of detail do you want?

Rephrase the above question as follows, and you are much more likely to be given the information you need:

> I have several questions about this subject, so I hope you won't mind if I take up some time just to get things straight in my mind. Firstly, please explain again what the purpose of the new school hall is.

Once you have received the reply to this question, you then move on to the latter questions, for example:

> Thank you. In that case, do you think that we have enough money to pay for the building?

If the answer to the above question is a straightforward 'yes' then the question regarding fundraising becomes irrelevant. This demonstrates the importance of putting your questions in a logical order so that time is not wasted ascertaining unnecessary information.

You may also have heard of **leading questions**. These are questions phrased in such a way that the person replying is pressured to agree with the theory being put forward. For example:

> It's correct, isn't it, that not building the school hall is the best solution to our problems?

If you listen to professional interviewers on the television and radio interviewing politicians and prominent businessmen, you will see how often they use leading questions to push their interviewee into making admissions or appearing aggressive.

Leading questions need to be handled carefully. They can be very helpful if the person being questioned has lost the thread of their argument and needs a little confidence-building to put them back on track. However, leading questions can, on occasion, be perceived as aggressive or antagonistic, especially if your respondent has to disagree with you. A further drawback with leading questions is that the other participants in the meeting may feel that you are steering the conversation down an agreed route rather than adhering to the rules of an open debate.

When asking questions, give your respondent adequate time to answer. He or she has to think of the answer—possibly even look up the information to be able to answer it—so be patient. If it is obvious that the person is in difficulties answering, an experienced Chair may help them out with some hints or suggestions. This is perfectly acceptable; unless you are intent on treating your respondent hostilely, accept the guidance of the Chair. Later in this chapter, tactics for disagreeing are discussed, but humiliating someone in a meeting is not constructive and tends to rebound on the aggressor.

Do!

listen to the answer to your question.

Don't!

assume that the answer will not make any difference to your original judgement.

When your respondent makes their reply, *listen* to their answer. 'Active listening' is a useful skill for meetings. This means absorbing and processing the information you receive. In this way you can base your next question or your final decision on what you hear at the meeting, and can amend any calculations you may have made before the meeting. For example, suppose you received a paper proposing a change to the management structure of a company in which you are a director. You may have thought before the meeting that this seems to be a logical step. From the information you gather at the meeting, you spot that the change is being proposed purely to oust a senior manager who is at loggerheads with another senior manager. In that case, the change is not useful to the company itself, and is really a personnel matter which should be handled quite differently.

Being questioned

Answering questions is one of the challenging aspects of taking an active part in a meeting. When you are the one in the firing line of questions, remember two things:

■ *Listen* to the question—don't assume you know what the question is before the enquirer has finished speaking. If you interrupt, this can be very irritating for the person asking the question and lead to confusion if you answer a question he or she was not asking in the first place. You also need to bring the powers of *active listening* into play again: listen for the message behind the question. The tone in which the question is asked and the language used can tell you a lot.

■ *Answer* the question—be precise when being asked a closed question and be positive when being asked an open question. If you are being asked a leading question, make sure that you do want to agree with it and take a moment to gather your thoughts if you need to disagree.

You may find it helpful to make notes as you are being queried, both of the question and of the facts or thoughts you need to include in your answer. It is polite to say to your questioner that you hope they won't mind if you take a few notes.

Just as you need to be prepared to change your point of view when you gather information, you also need to be ready to reach a compromise when you start to judge the mood of the meeting by the questions you are asked. Be prepared to have a couple of 'fallback' positions—and the information to support these—if you realize that your original proposal is not gaining wholehearted support.

Remember that no-one expects you to be a fluent, silver-tongued speaker, rolling out your case like Perry Mason. Try watching or listening to the debates in Parliament on the television or radio. If your view of debating is that it is like Prime Minister's Question Time, you will be quite surprised. The 'best' debating is done away from the glare of the media writers. Committees and debates in the House of Lords often give a much better picture of good debating. It's worth taking the time to listen and watch these debates to learn some of the skills of the trade.

If the Chair doesn't request participants to ask their questions one at a time, it is useful for the person taking questions to say so. It's surprising how many people think you can answer fourteen questions at the same time.

 Do!

take your time when answering questions: a rushed answer is often the wrong answer.

 Don't!

be pressurized into agreeing with a leading question: stand your ground.

Discussing

Now that we have been presented with the topic, and have questioned and clarified any points which were not clear, the discussion can really start.

Discussing is expressing your opinion, listening to others, and finding a way forward that suits the majority of the people at the meeting. Unless the action that the meeting needs to agree is very straightforward, most things agreed are a compromise. The meeting that can consistently find a compromise that is reasonable to everyone is rare, but it is what all meetings should strive towards. Later in this chapter we will talk about disagreements. While disagreements can be time-consuming and mean a lot of work for everybody, the meeting where everyone always agrees will be very dull and will have few new or exciting ideas. Discussion is therefore the lifeblood of a meeting and the part which gives it its special character.

*Discussing is ...
finding a way
forward.*

Expressing your opinion is a skill you need to build up. At early meetings, you may want to keep to simple agreements or rejections of proposals until you 'tune in' to the way that discussions are handled at your meeting. If you have a view you especially want to express, try taking rough notes of what you want to say with you to the meeting. The notes act to remind you of all the points you wanted to make and give you a 'safety net' of confidence; if you lose the thread of your point midway through, a quick glance at your notes will put you back on track. As you improve your skill your notes may consist of a few keywords. For instance, suppose you are a member of the local parish council, another member of which is keen that the council should support an application for planning permission to extend a listed building in the town. Your notes might read:

- Setting precedent for other buildings?

- New extension blocks light for neighbouring building.

- Where are construction lorries to park?

- Extension means cutting down hedgerow.

Remember, though, you may need to amend or even discard your notes altogether if the questions leading to the discussion have brought different facts and views to light.

If you start the debate on a proposal it's a good idea to state that you have x number of points to make, introduce them as 'firstly, secondly,' etc., and stick to that number. Avoid having more than four or five points to make, as this will be too much information for the meeting to take in.

If you enter the debate at a later point, make sure that you do not repeat points already made, although you could express your agreement or disagreement with them.

Some 'etiquette' points should be observed when there is an open debate:

4 Debating and discussing

The role of the Chair in guiding a discussion is key, and this will be discussed in the next chapter.

■ Don't interrupt others—unless you want them to interrupt you.

■ Respect the contribution each person makes: everyone at a meeting has been invited, appointed, or elected for the value they can bring to that meeting.

■ Keep to the point under discussion and don't veer off into side issues, especially personal issues.

■ If you refer to previous discussions, make sure that everyone knows what you are referring to, particularly new participants.

■ Avoid getting tangled up in very minor issues such as the spelling of a certain word or the date of another meeting: these are issues that can be more usefully solved outside the meeting.

■ Do not express an opinion on behalf of an absent participant unless you have their agreement, preferably in writing.

■ Unless you have professional qualifications, do not give a legal opinion on a constitutional issue.

Topics which should not be debated

There are subjects which meetings find it very difficult to debate sensibly and to reach a decision on. The most notorious of these is anything to do with design issues.

Design involves so many personal tastes that to design by committee is almost a guarantee of failure, as no compromise will ever suit everyone.

A camel is a horse designed by a committee

(Alec Issigonis)

Confidential matters such as pay or contractual terms can also be difficult matters for an open debate as the person affected may be present, or observers who should not be privy to the information. In this situation, the Chair can consider closing the meeting to observers and communicating the decisions made privately to the relevant people.

If you are in a new meeting situation, you will find other areas that crop up as time goes on where a consensus decision proves to be virtually impossible. In this case, the decision to be made is who should be given responsibility for looking after the area and reporting back as required to the meeting.

Proposing

After all the presenting, the information gathering and debating, you are at last in a position to make a proposal for action. The way proposals are made depends on how formal your meeting is. The Annual General Meeting of a company or association will have legal or constitutional procedures attached to the way a proposal is made, voted on, and agreed, while an informal meeting of a local campaigning group will simply agree to do something. In all cases, however, it is important that your proposal is clearly worded so that there can be no mistake in the action that is taken as a consequence of the agreement.

Proposals must be clearly worded to avoid future arguments.

All proposals should certainly be recorded in writing and kept safely, to avoid disputes and to act as a reference in the future.

In formal meeting situations, a **resolution** is made by a **proposer**. The resolution may be supported by a **seconder** and a vote of everybody at the meeting then taken. In trade unions and other membership societies, a proposal may have to be put to everyone who is a member by means of a postal ballot. Formal proposing and voting can take a long time, but it is vital to ensure that the democratic way the association carries out its business is maintained.

You may find it useful to draft a complicated proposal before a meeting and use that draft as the basis of discussion. Suppose that you want your Residents' Association committee to replace the existing entryphone system with a video entryphone system. Your original draft proposal might read:

The Residents' Association committee proposed to replace the current door entryphone system with a video entryphone system.

In the course of the discussion, members on the committee raise queries about costs and whether all the residents in the block would want to have the new system installed. As the meeting progresses and queries are raised, you would redraft your proposal to take them into account. Your final proposal reads:

Subject to the costs not exceeding £50 per resident and the agreement of a majority of the residents, the Residents' Association committee proposed to replace the current door entryphone system with a video entryphone system.

The only problem with this proposal is that it is still unclear who will be responsible for finding out costs and the wishes of the other residents, so you will need to add another explanatory paragraph to confirm the details.

Disagreeing

As mentioned above, a meeting which never has disagreements will rapidly stagnate through lack of new ideas and impetus. On the other hand, a meeting which has nothing but disputes will be just as useless. It is important to ensure that disagreements always have a constructive outcome. This calls for a certain amount of diplomacy on the part of participants.

Find the balance.

In practice this means that when you decide to disagree with a suggestion you should:

■ try to find an alternative way forward;

■ be courteous in disagreeing: outright confrontations rarely result in a constructive result;

■ check the reasons why you or others are disagreeing: are these based on a misunderstanding of the facts, a 'gut reaction', or genuine information?

■ not make a disagreement a personal issue.

Where all think alike, then no one thinks very much.
(Walter Lippmann)

A frequent cause of disagreement is the irrelevance or inappropriateness of a proposed action to the organization.

The most frequent causes of disagreement are discussed below. You will probably find others which are peculiar to your meeting: it is worth looking out for these over the course of several meetings and seeing how they might be avoided.

If you support the principle behind a suggestion but not the way it should be carried out, look for an alternative means of implementation. If you disagree with the principle, have positive reasons for disagreeing, such as the fact that the principle conflicts with the reason why the meeting (or organization itself) exists. Disagreements caused by such conflicts are very common, and point to an underlying need to spell out again the aims of the meeting, or organization.

Another common reason for disagreements is money: the costs involved in an action are too great. Look again for a positive angle. If you can support the principle, encourage the person who made the suggestion to seek ways to cut the cost or find means of financial backing. Or is it again an underlying trend—nothing can ever really be achieved because there is never enough money? In this case your meeting needs to spend more time addressing this root cause for disagreements.

New ideas and ways of doing things are another cause for disagreement. People are very hesitant to make big changes which can radically affect the way things have been done for a long time. Although 'If it ain't broke, don't mend it' is a good maxim, sometimes it can be difficult for people at the centre of things to take a balanced view and appreciate how the matter looks to an outsider. Positive encouragement is again the key to handling someone who meets every suggestion for change with a flat 'no'; ask them to give the new way of doing something a six-month trial, for example.

Personality clashes between participants involved in a meeting can also lead to disagreements. Such disagreements are especially destructive to the meeting, as other participants become bored by the time wasted by the routine argument between two participants. These situations are difficult to resolve without losing one or other of the participants, but a strong Chair may, by talking privately to the warring participants, be able to make them see that they are seriously hampering the work of the meeting.

Where participants are members of another organization or department, or have other vested interests in a particular course of action, this can make disagreements inevitable. It is worth spelling out that participants must give their sole attention to the business of the meeting and disregard external interests.

To be able to disagree in a meeting is a sign of confidence that you understand the subject under discussion and can put your case for not doing something. When you first start to attend meetings, you may find it easier to sound out other meeting members *before* a meeting to see who else might be disagreeing with an action. However, you should still attend the meeting with an open mind, and be prepared to listen and make your judgement on the outcome of the debate at the meeting.

Outright quarrels at meetings are rare, and are usually caused by poor preparation when participants are not kept informed about a project, or by poor Chairing.

Buying into the decision

Once a meeting has discussed and agreed an action, it is very important that everyone attending the meeting supports the action outside the meeting, no matter how hard they argued against the action within the meeting. Doing so ensures that the meeting presents a united front and gives the decision appropriate authority. Not doing so means that a meeting eventually splits into factions which never agree about anything, and spends most of its time politicking.

My sad conviction is that people can only agree about what they're not really interested in.

(Bertrand Russell)

Keep an open mind.

Support the decision.

STAFF ROOM

Finance Committee meeting tonight, then?

Outright quarrels at meetings are rare.

The Chair might wish to emphasize this point at the meeting, asking that no-one make statements to, for example, staff or the press without referring to him or her. Staff in organizations are sensitive to an open or covert lack of unity from a controlling body, and this can lead to a demoralized and unproductive workforce. Similarly, the press can very quickly exploit divisions in a body: consider the furore every time an MP takes a different view from that of the party leader.

Supporting an action you do not fully agree with is one of the hardest parts of participating in a meeting. Check *why* you do not accept the action and why the majority of the meeting does. If you feel very strongly, ask if the matter can be reconsidered at the next meeting, when you can propose a different course of action. Otherwise, once outside the meeting room you must put your full support to the action. This means you should:

- not delay any part you may have been assigned in putting the action into force;

- not continue to argue about the matter in future meetings unless it is an agenda item;

- not contact other participants outside the meeting and complain to them;

- in a work situation, not complain to a senior manager in order to have the decision overturned.

There are always exceptions to this rule and where a case of potential mismanagement is involved, you will definitely need to take further action. These exceptions are very rare and you must be absolutely sure of your facts before taking further action.

Chairing a meeting

5

Introduction

The Chair has a crucial role in determining how successful a meeting is. A good Chair will ensure a meeting keeps to its purpose, follows the agenda, runs to time, encourages constructive debate, and makes sure that everyone who takes part feels valued.

There are therefore lots of different skills involved in chairing: communication, leadership, motivational ability, judgement, diplomacy. These cannot be acquired overnight and can take years to build up. As a general participant, look out for good chairing and learn from these experiences so that you are ready to be a successful Chair when your turn comes.

A Chair is surrounded by people who are there to help—the officers of the meeting and the other participants. Making a positive working relationship with them is a two-way process: you can use their experience and skills, while giving them the opportunity to develop their responsibilities and skills as meeting participants and advisers.

In this chapter, we look at these various aspects of being a Chair. Although obviously intended mainly for Chairs of meetings, as a participant you should find this chapter helpful to look out for tips to pass on and, perhaps, for when you yourself become a Chair. As an organizer, if you are looking for a Chair, this chapter should give you some hints as to the type of person you need to find and the duties that need to be considered when drawing up the job of Chair.

Knowing your responsibilities

As a Chair, you need to be clear what your role is and what you are expected to do. At established meetings, your role will probably be already defined by custom: though a change of Chair may also be a chance to review these customs. Where there is a written constitution for either the meeting or the organization, this may contain a list of what you are expected to do, how you must run a meeting, or how you are expected to behave in general.

Ensure that you know what the meeting is to achieve and therefore what the Chair needs to do to help those aims.

You should also be certain what the aims of the meeting itself are. The Chair's role is to ensure that these objectives are achieved. It is therefore important to find a Chair who is sympathetic to the aims and will be able to give them whole-hearted support. If you have any doubt that you will find your-self in conflict with the business of the meeting, you should refuse the Chair, however flattering the offer may seem.

When you are putting a new meeting together, you should consider what the Chair's responsibilities are to be. You need to think about:

■ *Writing the agenda:* This could be the responsibility of the Chair, assisted by an administrator. The Chair needs to decide what items should be included on the agenda to reach the broad aims of the meeting (see Chapter 2). In formal board situations, the Chief Executive of the organization generally suggests to the Chair what the agenda should include.

■ *The papers accompanying the agenda:* Again this could be a task for the Chair, or it could be the role of an administrator, with the Chair reading over the papers before they are sent out and clarifying any points with the administrator.

■ *Who should attend the meeting:* The Chair might initially decide whom to invite to the first meeting: in future meet-ings, other participants might suggest new meeting

The Chair should contact meeting members.

members. The Chair should be the person who contacts suggested new participants and invites them to attend. The Chair could also approach professional advisers to ask them to attend as observers.

■ *When the meeting should be held:* The Chair needs to decide on the date of the meeting taking into account (a) his/her own availability, (b) the availability of other participants and whether a meeting can usefully be held if a participant cannot make a date.

■ *Managing the meeting:* The Chair will decide how to run discussion sessions, select who will speak or ask questions, and sum up points made. The Chair may also delegate roles in the meeting (such as minute taking or timekeeping).

■ *Voting:* The Chair of a meeting generally has a casting vote in situations where there are equal numbers of votes for and against a proposal. This means that the Chair in effect has two votes. At some meetings, the Chair may be required not to vote at all to emphasize their neutral status. At AGMs, members who are unable to attend often appoint the Chair as their proxy and empower him or her to vote on their behalf.

Leadership is action, not position.

(Donald H. McGannon, quoted in *Quotations for our Time*, edited by Laurence Peter)

■ *Abandoning discussion of a topic:* The Chair should have the final decision on when a meeting should defer discussion of a topic to another meeting if there is stalemate in the discussion.

■ *Private discussion:* The Chair may have the power to decide that certain participants should leave the room when a topic is being discussed due to its sensitive nature. Participants asked to leave are usually observers, or they might be full participants whose behaviour requires correction: in extreme cases it might involve the dismissal of a member of the meeting or a member of staff.

■ *Disciplining meeting participants:* Never a pleasant part of the Chair's role, but it is important that participants who break the rules of a meeting are informed of their error.

■ *Signing any paperwork* involved in a meeting such as minutes and agendas. The agenda is often signed by the Committee or Company Secretary, but it can also be signed by the Chair. The agreed minutes of a formal meeting are always signed by the Chair.

Meetings may also decide to impose certain restrictions on a Chair to ensure they do not abuse their power. In commercial situations, Chairs may be banned from holding positions of responsibility or shares in similar or competing organizations. There may also be rules regarding the financial status of the Chair (for example, they must not be declared bankrupt). The physical and mental health of the Chair may also be referred to, and anyone declared unfit may be required to resign their position.

Remember that Chairs in companies and charities will have additional duties outside the meeting situation, such as:

■ negotiating with third parties such as major clients, professional advisers, and legal counsel on constitutional points;

■ representing the organization at business and social events such as exhibitions, press launches, and gala events;

■ attending training courses to update information or learn new skills, especially company law and updates on the industry or the business;

- arbitrating in disputes between staff: Chairs are often cited as the last court of appeal in grievance and disciplinary procedures;

- attending and speaking at industry, academic, or association conferences.

These responsibilities usually mean that considerable travel may be involved, within and outside the country.

The time factor is therefore very important for a Chair whose responsibilities are wide-ranging: commitments in other areas may be seriously disrupted by the demands of the role.

All the above shows that the Chair must be an experienced and confident person with excellent self-organization. When setting up a meeting for the first time, ask yourself if you are the best person to act as Chair. You might find it easier to appoint someone who has experience of chairing to guide you through the first year of the meeting's existence. Alternatively, you may decide to ask a well-known person to take on the role to give standing to your meeting.

Working with participants

As a Chair, you will find yourself working with a variety of people, from the participants of the meeting to the 'backroom' people who carry out the administration which makes a meeting happen. You need to establish a good working relationship with both sets of people. You are aiming to build a team who enjoy working together, work positively together, and gain personal enjoyment from the work.

When taking over the Chairmanship of a meeting, concentrate your first efforts on the officers of the meeting: the Vice-Chair, Committee Secretary, and Minutes Secretary. (See Chapter 1 for the list of who's who at meetings.)

Establish a working relationship with all participants.

- *Vice-Chair*: The Vice-Chair takes over the meeting and any other responsibilities of the Chair when the Chair cannot carry these out. For example, at a meeting the Chair may find it useful to stand down temporarily if he or she wants to put forward a proposal of his or her own. In this case, the Vice-Chair would take over. The Vice-Chair therefore needs to be fully briefed about everything that is happening, so that she or he can help guide the discussion from the floor of the meeting. The Chair and Vice-Chair must work closely together so that they understand exactly what is required from the meeting.

■ *Company or Committee Secretary:* The Company Secretary is often also Managing Director or Chief Executive of the organization, and is in charge of meeting administration. The Secretary is the organization's 'inside voice' for a Chair, and will often suggest an agenda topic for discussion to the Chair. The Secretary will also be able to brief the Chair about any legal obligations the meeting has, so it is doubly important to listen to the Secretary's advice.

■ *Minutes Secretary:* The Minutes Secretary is in charge of taking notes at the meeting and producing minutes afterwards. The Chair needs to ensure the Minutes Secretary takes down all the relevant remarks and votes at a meeting. The Chair may also want to stop the Minutes Secretary taking notes on occasion if a very sensitive or confidential remark is made.

Working with the general participants

From previous meetings, you will probably know the general participants, how they work in and contribute to meetings. As Chair, you need to work out a strategy to bring out the best in the participants, encouraging those who are shy of speaking up at meetings, and ensuring that everyone has a fair chance of being heard. Some simple rules to achieve this strategy are:

■ Value all contributions participants make, even if they seem irrelevant or foolish.

■ Keep the discussion to the point in hand.

■ Where a participant proposes an action which is turned down by the meeting, ensure this is done positively and that the participant is thanked for their work in putting the proposal together.

- Look for a role for every participant: these could include presenting, leading the questions, timekeeping, minuting, summing up, checking the meeting or organizational rules. Giving participants an active part to play encourages them to be 'stakeholders' in the meeting.

- Always introduce and welcome new participants at the beginning of the first meeting they attend.

- Use sub-committees as a way of encouraging less experienced participants to contribute. In a smaller meeting, people are generally less afraid to speak up.

Work out a strategy to bring out the best in all participants.

As you get to know your participants better, you will know their strengths and weaknesses. In Chapter 2, different types of people were discussed. Use these characteristics to the advantage of the meeting, and match participants' skills with the work that needs to be done. Don't, for example, ask a contributor to find out about a topic when a researcher will delight in the work and a contributor will hate it.

On the other hand, you need to be alive to the potential of participants who want to develop their skills. Purely because one person has always taken the minutes does not mean that another participant might not like to try minuting, while the minute taker would like to try presenting a proposal.

Managing the meeting

Obviously, your most important task as Chair is to run the meeting in a way that means the meeting is constructive, useful to the people it is aiming to help, and involves all the participants. You can help yourself achieve these aims by:

- knowing exactly what you want the meeting to do. Read all the paperwork, confer with the Secretary to see what he or she wants the meeting to achieve;

- discussing any controversial topics with key participants before the meeting to ensure they understand why the topic is being raised and to identify any concerns they have which may need to be addressed at the meeting by the proposer;

■ keeping to time in the meeting. Allot a time to each agenda item and try to ensure the meeting keeps to these times. It's a good idea to take your watch off and put it in front of you so that you stay aware of how the time is going. Tell participants that you want to give, say, twenty minutes to the open discussion of a topic. This helps to focus every-one's minds. Where the discussion starts to run over time but it is evident that this extra time is necessary, suggest deferring other less important items to the next meeting, or having a special meeting to discuss the topic where it is a major subject;

Keep to the matter in hand.

■ keeping the meeting to the matter in hand. Where you have participants who know each other well, it is easy to get diverted to other subjects. The odd digression is fine, but keep a firm hand on the discussion so that business comes first!

■ summarizing the discussion for participants. This keeps the pros and cons of a subject clear and makes it easier for the meeting to reach a decision;

■ using sub-committees as a way of keeping long, involved dis-cussions out of the main meeting. Sub-committees can do invaluable work in researching a complex topic and giving the main meeting just one or two recommendations, rather than the main meeting using up a lot of time in hearing many opinions;

To get something done a committee should consist of no more than three men, two of whom are absent.

(Robert Copeland)

■ being ready to change the way a meeting discusses its busi-ness. Meetings develop and change as the business they discuss changes, or participants get used to the way of meetings. Stay alert to ways in which the meeting can be improved and never be afraid to suggest amendments (as long as these are allowable under any constitutional or legal obligations). Be open, too, to suggestions from participants about changing the way the meeting runs: don't take such remarks personally but realize they are made for the good of the meeting;

■ making sure that decisions made at meetings are carried out. This is where a good relationship with the Secretary is important, so that you can contact him or her between meetings and ask about progress. Being approachable will encourage the Secretary to contact you if unforeseen difficulties crop up in the course of decisions being put into practice. You can then alert participants to delays or problems, demonstrating that you are in control of the situation.

When you chair a meeting, you are managing a team. Check out books and television programmes on team building and see if their ideas can be transferred to your meeting. Learn from the experience of those who have done it before: from trade union leaders to captains of industry.

The Industrial Society (website: www.indsoc.co.uk) and the Institute of Directors (website: www.iod.com) run a variety of courses on leadership issues. Hawksmere seminars may also have one- and two-day courses appropriate to your needs (website: www.hawksmere.co.uk).

Think about occasionally having a team-building exercise at a meeting, or devoting a special meeting to a series of these exercises. Such exercises can be especially effective at a newly set up meeting where participants do not know each other well.

See page 127 in Part B for examples of team-building exercises.

Disagreements and discipline

Meetings do not always run smoothly. Participants fall out, proposals are controversial, a participant may do something wrong and require disciplining. It is the Chair's duty to make sure that disagreements are sorted out positively and that breaches of discipline are resolved with the least damage to both the meeting and the organization.

Anticipating trouble before it happens is one way to ensure that serious disagreements are kept to a minimum. I have already said that contacting participants before a meeting to discuss any potentially problematic subjects is a good idea. At the meeting, when serious arguments arise, you have several options:

 Do!

meet trouble before it happens by keeping up good communications with participants.

 Don't!

expect that the meeting will always run smoothly: argument is healthy if constructive.

■ Take a break: giving participants a ten-minute break to walk away from the meeting, have a coffee, etc. can be very effective in calming tempers and encouraging a more positive atmosphere.

■ Take the meeting into an **in camera** session: 'in camera' is the Latin phrase for a private meeting, to which only certain participants are invited. In practice this means that all observers and most officers are asked to leave the meeting, while full participants discuss the topic between themselves. This can be helpful, as participants sometimes feel freer to express themselves in a smaller meeting, or when non-participants are not present. It is essential to do this when disciplining a participant or officer, to minimize embarrassment all round.

■ Enforce a 'guillotine' on the discussion by stating that there is, for example, ten minutes left for a decision to be reached. Follow this by recapping the points made and the alternative proposals. This focuses participants on the real issues and gives them a pause to reflect while you speak.

■ Defer the discussion to a separate meeting, and ask for additional information to be prepared to help everyone make a balanced and rational decision.

Do!

take prompt action when a participant is in error.

Don't!

discipline in front of others unless unavoidable, but inform participants that the error has been noted and corrected.

One of the most difficult meeting situations is the disciplining of members of staff or meeting participants. These situations tend to happen when participants have:

■ overstepped their responsibility and carried out an action they were not authorized to do;

■ breached the confidence of the meeting and told people outside the meeting what has taken place;

■ failed to carry out an action agreed by a meeting.

Again, the key is to try and make sure these situations do not arise by making it clear, when decisions are taken, who must do what by when, and who may be told about decisions. If, however, a situation requiring disciplinary action does arise, the Chair should first contact the person who has made the error, to see why it happened.

Quite often, it is a genuine error on the part of the participant and a simple verbal rap over the knuckles by the Chair is enough to stop any further mistakes.

Wilful breaches of a meeting's etiquette or intentional overstepping of responsibilities are more serious. Where an organization has a disciplinary system, this should then be followed. Where no system has been set up, a decision needs to be taken about what action should be taken—this may be a letter to the participant, pointing out the error and informing them that any further breaches will lead to their dismissal from the meeting.

It is important that action is always taken when a disciplinary offence occurs. This shows that the meeting is serious and that it has taken constructive action to stop the error. Simply ignoring a breach of discipline is never acceptable, as it undermines the whole ethos of the meeting and stores up more trouble for the future.

Tip
Sometimes a meeting fails to reach a decision but continually defers an issue from meeting to meeting. As the Chair you may decide that the meeting *has* decided: 'not to decide is to decide,' writes Harvey Cox. Try removing the issue from the agenda and merely reporting it as an issue with 'no further progress'. Although this is frustrating for the proposer, it makes more sense to inform him or her privately that the issue has been removed until the meeting can see a more positive time for it to be dealt with.

6 | Minutes

Introduction

Minutes are a record of what happened at a meeting. They are important, as they remind participants what actions they need to take as a result of discussions and show the process which led up to the decision—which often reflects how the meeting wants the action carried out.

Minutes also serve a useful historical purpose: future meetings can refer to them for information on previous discussions and decisions.

There is a legal requirement for signed minutes to be kept by organizations who are governed by company or charity legislation.

Taking minutes involves listening and the ability to write clearly and concisely, while still giving the 'feel' and character of a meeting and its participants.

In this chapter the basic building blocks of taking minutes are considered. From these you can evolve your own style and way to make minute-taking easy. There is a mistaken belief that a Minutes Secretary *must* have shorthand: although this is helpful, it is perfectly possible to train yourself to take longhand minutes by listing key points and using abbreviations which you will find yourself developing over the course of several meetings.

If you are not currently responsible for the minutes, you may still find this chapter useful for the future; see if there are any tips you can pass on to the current Minutes Secretary of your meeting.

The Minutes Secretary

The person who takes minutes is known formally as a Minutes Secretary. It is this person's responsibility to take notes of a meeting's discussion and decisions. The Secretary writes up these notes into a formal document and distributes them to all the participants. The Secretary may assist the Committee Secretary in preparing and sending out the agenda and accompanying papers, and be responsible for any administrative matters during a meeting, The Minutes Secretary should keep a file of all past meeting papers and minutes, so that these can be easily referred to at any time.

The role of Minutes Secretary is often combined with another role: for example, a general participant may be responsible for taking the minutes. This works well until the participant is called upon to speak, as it is difficult to talk and take minutes. It can therefore be useful, in meetings where the minute-taker plays an active role, to have a 'reserve' minuter who will take over when the Secretary is engaged in the discussion.

A Minutes Secretary needs to develop the following skills:

- *Listening skills:* Listen to what people actually say, not what you think they say.

- *Learning the way participants talk:* Knowing the way participants express themselves helps minute-taking.

- *Alertness:* You must be constantly alert during the meeting. Don't rely on someone else remembering what was said!

- *Rapport with the Chair of the meeting:* Build a good relationship with the Chair of the meeting, so that you know what they want from the Minutes, and, in meetings, you can signal to them that you have not been able to minute an item if the discussion is going too fast!

- *Distancing:* Remain an impartial witness to proceedings. Do not become involved with the discussion unless you are a participant combining the role of Minutes Secretary with other duties.

Listen to what people say, not what you think they say.

■ *Confidentiality:* A Minutes Secretary is in a position of trust, privy to confidential information. You should never discuss anything said at a meeting with anyone who was not present. If you are concerned by issues discussed, talk to someone who was at the meeting.

You should never discuss anything said at a meeting.

Types of minute

Examples of these types of minute are given in Part B, on pages 130–2.

The type of minutes you take depend on the meeting. An informal meeting can be minuted in a brief email to everyone who was there, but a formal meeting will require structured minutes, as we will discuss next.

Informal minutes can be:

Email is an ideal medium for communicating informal minutes.

■ a bullet point list of decisions taken or progress on work to date;

■ a list in table format, giving the topic, the decision made or progress to date, and the next action to be taken;

■ a narrative report of a conversation that took place between several people.

Formal minutes may be:

■ minimal: often a single side of A4 giving the bare minimum of information on who was present, when and where, and details of resolutions passed. Often used for a small company's minutes where formal meetings are held infrequently and are concerned only with legislative requirements;

■ medium: a structured report with headings, giving a précis of what was said at a meeting. The most usual form of minutes, giving details of discussions and the reasoning leading up to a decision;

■ verbatim: a word-for-word account of what was said. Although unusual, these are in use. Hansard, the record of the debates in the Houses of Commons and Lords, is an example.

When taking on the role of Minutes Secretary, look at the minutes of previous meetings for the preferred style. If you see places where improvements can be made, make the suggestion to the Committee Secretary or Chair. If you are minuting a new meeting, try out various styles of minutes to see which best suits the meeting. Ask the Chair for feedback from participants, then adjust them to be useful to everyone.

Structure of minutes

As with reports and papers, minutes need to be structured so that they are easy for participants to follow. The structure is determined to some extent by the agenda of the meeting, as minutes will follow the discussion of its items. However, there are some sections to be added to the framework that the agenda provides. The following list gives the most usual examples of these: your own meeting may have extras it likes to include.

■ *date, time and place of the meeting*

■ *purpose or title of the meeting*
For example, 'Committee meeting', 'Management meeting' etc.

■ *who was there and their position/status at the meeting*
A record of the attendees at a meeting is extremely important for accountability reasons. Participants who are not present may disagree with a decision taken in their absence,

Try out various styles of minutes.

Committee: a group of men who keep minutes and waste hours.
(Milton Berle)

In Part B, page 132, you will find a template structure for minutes based on a typical agenda.

and need to be able to state in future that they were not present. Alternatively, participants need, on occasion, to be reminded that they were present when a decision is taken which they later decide they do not like!

The usual way to list people is to start with the name of the Chair of the meeting, followed by the comment '(Chair)', then the rest of the participants in alphabetical order. Define clearly whether people were full participants or observers by listing the full participants first, then a list of other attendees, headed 'In Attendance'.

You also need to note down if participants or observers were present only for a certain item, or if they left before the end of the meeting.

■ *Who was absent*
A list of absentees is generally given under the first agenda item, 'Apologies for absence'. This is again a vital piece of information to show that the person was not party to information given out at the meeting or to votes taken on a proposal.

The Minutes Secretary may receive notice from a participant that he/she will not be attending; if no prior warning is received, the participant's name is still noted under 'Apologies for absence'. The Minutes Secretary should inform the Chair, discreetly, that no notice was received, so that the Chair can pursue this matter with the participant if he or she wishes.

All the above items are standard to any meeting. One very important item for the Minutes Secretary is:

■ *Minutes of the last meeting and signing*
The minutes of the last meeting are considered for factual or grammatical errors. Some participants prefer to communicate any amendments to the Minutes Secretary prior to the meeting. It will then be up to the Secretary to inform the meeting of the proposed change. Alternatively, participants may wish to raise matters at the meeting itself. The amendment should be read out in the wording in which the participant wants the minute to read. A vague remark such as 'I don't think the item about salaries is very clear' is not acceptable.

See Chapter 3 for other items which may be included in an agenda, such as adoption of the agenda and appointment of a Chair.

It is up the Chair to press this point with the participant and ask for a redraft of the minute in question. If the Chair is not very confident or experienced, the Minutes Secretary should ask (politely) how the participant would like the minute to read.

Once amendments have been made, the minutes are signed by the Chair. The Minutes Secretary should have a copy of the minutes ready for the Chair to sign. This action is always recorded in the minutes, and legally signifies that everyone accepts the minutes.

> Always make sure you receive back the signed copy of the minutes. These can be easily mislaid in a meeting with lots of papers lying about. At the end of the meeting, file the signed minutes in a safe place as soon as possible.
>
> Signed minutes must be kept in a way which allows them to be inspected on demand by any participant, the company auditors, industry regulators, shareholders, or other authorized people. They can be written in or appended to the Company Register (if relevant), or kept in a separate file in date order.

Preparing to take minutes

In keeping with one of the recurring themes of this book, advance preparation is one of the keys to helping yourself take good minutes. A couple of days before your meeting, run through the following list for useful background information.

In Part B, page 132, you will find a template structure for minutes based on a typical agenda.

■ Ask for a **list of participants**: check what each person's role is, or if they are from an external organization. Also check the voting rights of each participant so that you do not inadvertently include them if there is a vote at the meeting.

■ Ask for a copy of **the agenda** and any **papers** which accompany the agenda. The more information you have about what will be discussed, plus the jargon, acronyms, names of people, and companies which will be used, the better your minutes will be, as you will have an understanding of what is being discussed and know the terms and names which will crop up. Looking back through previous minutes can also help you see what the current stage of discussion is on any topic. For example, is this a new issue, a subject always discussed, or a one-off?

Advance preparation is one of the keys to taking good minutes.

■ Ask for a copy of any drafts of formal **resolutions** in advance
Resolutions often have a particular legal wording, so having
an advance copy ensures that you have the correct wording.
Be warned, though—the wording might be changed at the
meeting, so stay alert.

■ Ask if there will be any **presentations** and if you can have a
hard copy of these. This will save you minuting them in full.
In your written-up minutes, a summary of presentations is
all that is needed.

See Chapter 5 for *in camera* sessions.

■ Ask **how the meeting will be run**. Will there be an *in camera*
session? Will there be a change of Chair mid-way through the
meeting? Are there any papers that will be tabled?

The other things that you can do to help yourself are:

■ Make sure you have **the right equipment**: use a bound notebook rather than loose sheets of paper, so as to avoid losing
a sheet, or muddling the order of the papers. Also, always
take two pens to a meeting—take just one and it's guaranteed to run out.

Keep it confidential!

At the end of a meeting, collect any papers that have been left behind by participants and either keep them safe to return to participants or destroy them.

Tabled papers are sometimes strictly confidential. Make sure you destroy them securely after you have finished referring to them.

■ Make sure you have all the relevant papers: you should have:
  ○ a copy of the agenda and papers;
  ○ a copy of the last meeting's minutes for signature. You
    might also want to have another copy on which to write
    amendments which crop up in the course of the agenda
    item 'Minutes of the last meeting', to refer to during
    'Matters arising', and to keep for your own records;
  ○ your list of the participants;
  ○ a note of any apologies for absence;
  ○ any amendments to be made to the previous minutes;
  ○ a diary (helps when setting the date of the next meeting).

During the meeting, make sure you receive a copy of
any papers which are tabled for when you write up
your minutes.

- Arrive promptly at the meeting so that you have time to settle yourself and lay out your papers. Find yourself a seat near to the Chair where there is enough room to write comfortably. If there is no table, take a clipboard or a large book to rest your notebook on as you write.

6 Minutes

- Ask someone to point out who's who at the meeting and make a sketch map for yourself of who is sitting where. A quick glance at your sketch map will remind you during the meeting who is speaking if you get lost. Check the spelling of the names of any participants who are not familiar to you.

See Part B, page 133 for an example of a sketch map.

Depending on the role of the Minutes Secretary, you may also be responsible for the following:

- Timekeeping at the meeting: have a watch in front of you so that you can time discussions and tell the Chair if time is running out.

- Liaising with the venue regarding refreshments, seating arrangements, setting up equipment for presentations: if so, arrive at least half an hour before the meeting to deal with any last-minute hitches. If you are involved in setting up the room, arrive an hour earlier.

- Bringing in observers or advisers to the part of the meeting relevant to them: make sure you know where these people will be waiting.

Taking minutes

Taking minutes is a matter of taking notes of what is being said. Your aim is to get the gist of a discussion, information points, and decisions. Concentration is vital. Unless you have shorthand, you will normally be minuting a sentence or two behind what is actually being said, and good participants will take this into account, speaking reasonably slowly, or repeating their point. As you get used to the way people speak, you will find minuting easier. You will know, for example, that John Brown begins by recapping things that have been said before (so you don't really need to note them again) and leaves

There is no right or wrong way to take minutes: everyone has their own style.

If you are a fast typist, you might try using a laptop computer to take minutes.

his point to the end. On the other hand, Helen Smith always asks a question or makes her point right away, so you need to start writing as soon as she speaks.

One way to practise taking minutes is to minute news or factual radio or television programmes. Start by taking notes of a report by a single journalist and build up to whole conversations. If you have the facility to record a programme, compare your notes to the recording to see how accurate you were. When you can minute the whole of *Question Time* you will be a Minutes Secretary *par excellence*. Another way to improve your ability to summarize and recall conversations is to keep a diary, logging one conversation each day.

The two trickiest passages to minute are (a) an open discussion and (b) an argument (discussed later in this chapter). You will probably find that the remarks made in an open discussion do not follow on from each other, and participants may jump back to a remark made earlier. Leave lines in between each noted remark so that you have space to add in extra comments.

On page 133 of Part B you will find an example of notes of an open discussion.

You will find you develop your own shorthand as your skills develop. For example, use the initials of participants in your notes, rather than full names, but look out if participants have the same initials! Remember that your notes are for your use: it doesn't matter if they are messy or don't make sense to anyone else—as long as you understand them. There is no right or wrong way to take minutes: everyone has their own style.

Writing up minutes

Aim to write up minutes within one week of a meeting taking place. After this, your memory of what happened tends to fade.

An example of this is given on page 130 of Part B.

A good way to start writing up minutes is to **draw up a blank table** containing all the headings and sub-headings which you then fill in. Splitting up minutes into sections makes them easier to tackle.

Decide on the **grammatical style** in which you will write your minutes. In formal minutes, the past tense is usually used. Bullet point style minutes are in the present tense.

If you are writing up minutes on a word processor, writing your minutes in table format makes it simpler to lay out sub-headings or clauses under sub-headings. If you are using a typewriter, set your tabs before you start so that you don't have to worry about them half way through your document.

Include **page numbers** to help participants locate minutes they wish to refer to when discussing them at a subsequent meeting. 'At the top of page 4' is much easier to find than 'the page which starts with the paragraph about time management'.

You do not have to stick rigidly to the headings of the agenda: add in **sub-headings** if you feel that this will help to clarify the minutes. Suppose there was an agenda item called 'Computer systems', but the meeting actually discussed the progress made with the new computer system and the new website, and a number of remarks were also made about problems with emailing the organization. You could therefore write up the minutes for this item using the following structure:

Do remember to save as you go, and make a back-up on floppy disk.

2. <u>**Computer systems**</u>

2.1:   New computer system

2.2:   Website

2.3:   Email facility

Another issue you need to decide is whether to write up minutes in chronological or logical order. In an open discussion session, participants jump backwards and forwards from one topic to another. Try grouping remarks together to make the minutes understandable, rather than noting them in the exact order in which they were said.

On page 133 of Part B, you will find examples of written-up minutes of an open discussion.

The same issue applies to meetings where agenda items were not discussed in their original order. This may have been because the participants needed to discuss the item were not present at the time the meeting reached that point. Check with the Chair what order they want the minutes in.

If an agenda item was not discussed at all, because events had moved on subsequent to the agenda being drawn up, you will need to note this in your minutes, for example: 'Discussion on

Pages 135–6 of Part B gives an example of the handwritten notes of an argument and the written-up minutes.

this item was deferred until the next meeting' or 'It was decided that this item was no longer relevant.' It may seem strange to note that no discussion took place, but future meetings need to know why the discussion was abandoned.

Writing up an argument at a meeting calls for a certain amount of tact. Unless you are writing the meeting up word for word, do not minute insults, flat contradictions, or any of the rest of the phases of an argument. Your minutes should make clear there was a disagreement, without going into detail.

There are some stock phrases that you can use when writing up a disagreement:

■ *'After discussion it was agreed that …'* This bypasses the argument altogether. As you attend more meetings, you will begin to know when this is acceptable, or if the participants will want more detail.

■ *'The meeting was surprised to note …'* Conveys some anxiety and tension.

■ *'There was some disagreement with this view and the following remarks were made …'* You would follow this up with an impersonal bullet point list of the remarks.

You can never smooth over everything. It will be very obvious on occasion that participants are furious and you then have to make this clear in the minutes. If, however, the argument becomes very heated and acrimonious, it is quite possible that the Chair will decide to take the meeting 'in camera' and ask you to stop minuting.

Retain your impartiality in your minutes.

So shall I minute that as the decision wasn't unanimous?

You need to remember that you must stand outside the 'business' of the meeting. You are an impartial witness, and you need to retain that impartiality in your minuting. However supportive or otherwise you are of remarks made by participants, do not let your own feelings show in your minutes.

The Minutes Secretary must remain an impartial witness.

Other tips for minute writing

Abbreviations: As you write your minutes, make the last page of your document a list of abbreviations and what they stand for. Add to your list as you write the minutes. You could also include an explanation of any technical terms which were used. You may find it helpful to construct in a separate document a master list of all abbreviations and technical terms used by the meeting and then copy across the relevant ones to your current minutes. This will also help you to remember what, for example, BVF does stand for, without having to ask others.

Include a list of abbreviations and jargon used in the minutes to help readers understand them.

Action points: A list of the agreed actions and who is to do what can be useful as a quick reference point. Include the list at the end of the minutes.

See page 136 for examples of action point templates.

Items for the next agenda: Help the Chair or Committee Secretary by keeping a list of items which participants asked to be included on the agenda of the next meeting.

Read it over: When you finish writing the minutes, leave them on one side for a while and then read them back to yourself. You will inevitably spot mistakes you would otherwise miss.

Wise after the event? It sometimes happens that events move so quickly that minutes become obsolete within days. Avoid the temptation, based on your knowledge of an event, to discard a minute or alter what was said because you know things have changed; these things will be picked up and explained at the next meeting.

If you are writing minutes on a word-processor, print them out and read them through. You often miss errors on the screen which are obvious on the page.

Presenting minutes

When you finish writing up, you should send the minutes to the Chair of the meeting and/or the Committee Secretary for checking. You may be asked to send draft minutes to other participants for their comments, especially legal advisers who will need to verify the wording of any resolutions that were agreed.

 Do!

give participants a deadline for submitting amendments to the minutes.

 Don't!

take amendments personally. Everyone misunderstands or misinterprets remarks.

Do not start to make any amendments until you receive everyone's feedback. You can then amalgamate all the suggested changes into one document. If one participant has amended a minute in one way and another in another, refer to the Company Secretary or Chair for a final ruling. If you are genuinely unhappy with an amendment, discuss this with the Chair. You should certainly stand your ground if you are asked to take out or alter an amendment; this is manipulation of facts and you should not be party to it.

Once the minutes are complete, print out or photocopy enough copies for all the participants. If appropriate, give these to the Committee Secretary ready for sending out.

The right time to send out minutes varies from organization to organization and from meeting to meeting. The Chair may ask you to send out minutes as soon as he or she has checked them. Meetings of company board meetings are generally sent out with the agenda for the following meeting. Minutes of AGMs will not be sent out until the following year. This means that you must have a very carefully arranged procedure for the safe keeping of the minutes, and must know where to find them twelve months after you wrote them.

Traditionally, minutes have been kept in paper format. The growth of computing offers some alternatives (although you will still need at least one hard copy for signature). These include:

- email: useful for circulating draft minutes quickly to participants for checking;

- shared document folder or Intranet: where participants are logged into the same network and share documents, setting up a folder—preferably password protected—gives easy access at all times. It also saves individual participants having to devise their own storage system;

- Extranet: An Extranet is an extension of the shared document folder where external participants also have the ability to log on to an organization's network. Care needs to be taken with confidentiality and virus protection.

Do!
remember to keep back a copy of the minutes ready for signing at the next meeting.

Don't!
send out minutes to all participants until they have been agreed by the Chair.

Exploit the possibilities of the latest ways of sending and keeping documents to speed up circulating minutes and to simplify storage.

Following up 7

Introduction

For meetings to have any credibility, decisions made at them must be put into practice. Meeting participants need to be able to keep a check on what is being done. Without this follow-up to a meeting, all meetings will be just talking-shops, without interest to the people they should be serving.

This chapter considers ways to keep track of decisions and how to ensure they are carried out. The chapter is for both organizers and participants, as it provides information to help you work out a way to ensure the decisions of a meeting are implemented and to measure the progress of the implementation.

Dividing up the decision

Every time a decision is made by a meeting, it is not enough to just decide to do something; participants must also decide the following points:

■ Who is to be responsible for the action?

■ Who is to carry out the action? This is not always the same as being responsible for the action. For example, the Chair might be responsible for the action, but the Committee Secretary will do any practical work that is required. Other people not at the meeting may also be needed to carry out parts of the decision; check that someone will inform them and coordinate the work they will be doing.

■ When the action must be completed. Having a time schedule and a deadline makes sure that the person responsible for carrying out the action can build the action into their own personal timetable.

Break down a decision into single elements to minimize confusion.

Do!
allow sufficient time
for the decision to be
put into practice.

 Don't!
forget to ask for an
interim report to
make sure progress
is being made.

On page 136 of Part
B you will find an
example of an action
point template.

Use an email to
inform a number of
people of a decision
taken by a meeting.
This is a quick
method of
communicating.
Further, the email
can be saved and
referred to in the
future in case of
any query.

■ Who is to report back to the meeting and at which meeting they must report. Long-term actions may take more time to complete than the time between one meeting and the next; decide a fair time-frame. You might ask for an interim report at the next meeting and a final report at the following meeting.

■ What individual tasks are involved in carrying out the decision? Decisions rarely involve just one job: several things may need to happen for the whole decision to have been accomplished.

■ Who is to inform people not at the meeting of the decision if it affects them? This could involve a press release to the general public if you are involved in a decision made at local government level, or a letter to parents if you are a school governor.

Keeping track of all the elements which make up a decision is important, and one way to do this is to produce an action point list with each set of minutes. Action points should be distributed to everyone involved in carrying out a decision, whether or not they were at the meeting. Action points should therefore be on a separate piece of paper so that confidential minutes are not included with the list.

As an example of dividing up a decision, suppose the board of a company has authorized the purchase of new software for the company. Putting this decision into practice means:

■ The Chief Executive has overall responsibility for the project. The Chief Executive will brief the Systems Manager and Finance Manager on what the board has agreed, including the budget and the timescale.

■ The Systems Manager will be responsible for obtaining quotations for the software, deciding on the supplier, and authorizing payment by the Finance Manager. The Systems Manager will also inform all the staff of what is going to happen and arrange any training required.

■ The Systems Manager will provide an interim report on progress for the Chief Executive to include in her report at the next meeting.

Sub-committees

Sometimes a sub-committee is appointed by the main meeting to discuss a particular topic. These could include:

- design issues: new logo and stationery;

- financial issues: setting or reviewing a budget;

- staff benefits: pensions, private medical care, and other insurance schemes;

- business development: brainstorming potential new areas of business;

- special events: conferences, campaigns.

When the main meeting sets up a sub-committee, the decision needs to consists of:

- Who is to be on the sub-committee. If anyone outside the meeting is appointed to the sub-committee, it should also be decided who is to approach these people and invite them to take part in the sub-committee. Decide also if anyone else should be told about the sub-committee.

- What the exact brief of the sub-committee is. If the sub-committee is considering a budget, the brief would be (a) to receive the draft budget and consider it, (b) to make any amendments and ask for the budget to be redrafted with these amendments, (c) when the final draft is ready, to prepare a presentation on the budget for the main meeting, and (d) to present the budget at the meeting to be held on such-and-such a date.

- Whether the sub-committee is formed for one specific purpose or if it should continue until the main meeting decides to disband it.

- Whether the sub-committee has any powers of decision or if it can only make recommendations to the main meeting.

Do!

use a sub-committee to process issues with a lot of information.

Don't!

have so many sub-committees that there are more meetings being held than core work happening.

Be clear what the task of the sub-committee is, and make sure that all the participants are fully informed and understand it too.

I think he's misunderstood what a sub-committee is.

Reporting

Keep track of what is happening.

Reporting is the way a meeting keeps track of what is happening.

At each meeting, one item on the agenda should always be 'Actions since last meeting' or 'Matters arising' (see Chapter 3). At this point in the meeting, participants in charge of decisions and projects should give a progress update. Participants should refer to the action points of each meeting and request a progress report if they are not covered elsewhere in the meeting. The person in charge of each action can give either a verbal or written report. Any problems with progress should be highlighted and, if necessary, the timetable or costs involved can then be revised.

See Page 136 of Part B for an example template for this list.

Where an action is not finished between meetings, you might choose to have an 'Outstanding action points' list which sets out progress to date and the work left to do.

Finishing off

A report of the whole project can be helpful for future meetings to decide how to run projects, especially if the project went particularly well—or badly. Your final report should include:

Do!

remember to inform the meeting when a decision has been carried through and is complete.

Don't!

forget to thank the people who put the decision into practice.

- the names of everyone involved and any thanks you would like to give them;

- costs involved and whether these were under or over budget (and if so, why);

- any future actions which could enhance the project or build on its success.

Participants at meetings can show their thanks to the people who carried out the project in various ways such as minuting thanks, a financial gratuity, or a present. If thanks are minuted, remember to make it someone's responsibility to inform the person of these thanks.

Troubleshooting 8

Introduction

In an ideal world every meeting runs smoothly, participants make constructive comments, and everyone looks forward to attending a meeting. Unfortunately, such meetings are rare.

Throughout the book, suggestions for how to solve some of the problems which arise in meetings have been given. This chapter looks at two more general areas where problems arise: problems for participants and problems with the meeting in general.

Problems participants find in attending meetings are discussed first, then problems with the meeting itself, mainly aimed at Chairs and organizers. As a participant you may still find the second part useful, as you could raise the suggestions it contains as an agenda item or have a private talk about them with the Chair; you may be surprised to find that the Chair has not realized how participants feel. If you are the Chair of the meeting, it is important to listen to such suggestions and accept them as proof that your meeting members *want* the meeting to succeed, rather than taking it as a personal criticism.

This chapter has been written in a problem-and-solution format, which should help you identify your particular problem and its solution at a glance. You will also find 'problem buster' boxes in this chapter: short suggestions for solving at least part of the problem.

Participants' problems

I don't like talking in front of people

Think about 'meeting' situations where you are relaxed.

If this is your reason for not liking meetings, think back to the very first sentence of this book: every time you say 'hello' you start a meeting. You are involved in 'meetings' all the time—even talking on the telephone is a meeting.

To help you overcome the fear of talking in front of others, think about 'meeting' situations where you are relaxed, for example, chatting with friends, discussing items with an assistant in a shop, talking over an issue at work with a colleague. You may find these situations easier because you know what you are going to say and know all about the subject you are discussing. If you prepare for a meeting by reading all the reports and papers, you will be in the same position. If there is something you don't understand, don't be afraid to have an informal chat with another person who attends the meeting to ask them to explain, perhaps the Chair or the Committee Secretary.

You can also give yourself confidence by taking time to get used to a meeting. Don't feel you must say something straight away at your first meeting—a lot of meetings become boring and reach no decisions when everyone feels they must make their presence felt. Listen to the discussion and take part if you strongly object or strongly agree. You need not say anything at all. A good Chair might ask you to give your opinion if you haven't spoken during a debate, but again, all you need to begin with is an expression of agreement or rejection.

Once you have been to a meeting and you know what happens and who else is there, you will start to feel you can—and want to—contribute.

PROBLEM BUSTER

Block out time in your diary not just to attend the meeting but to prepare for it. You will be much more positive about going to meetings if you read the reports in advance, understand the issues to be discussed, and note down questions to be asked.

I've been asked to give a presentation at a meeting but I feel very unsure about it

If you are making a presentation to a meeting, it can be useful to have a rehearsal and give the presentation to someone you know and trust, such as a friend or family member. Ask them to give you constructive comments. Does the presentation make sense? Is it too short or too long? Can they understand you—are you speaking slowly and loudly enough? Most people tend to speed up when speaking if they are nervous, and their voice will also be quieter than usual.

If you are using a visual aid, whether it is an overhead projector or a computer-based slide presentation, have a run-through with it first so that you are sure you know how the equipment works. If you have time at the meeting, make sure the equipment is working properly: nothing is more calculated to switch off people's interest than delays while you search for a plug socket!

I am the most spontaneous speaker in the world because every word, every gesture and every retort has been carefully rehearsed.

(George Bernard Shaw)

PROBLEM BUSTER

Take two deep breaths before you start to speak—and smile! Smiling relaxes the facial muscles and gives you your normal tone and volume of speech.

I haven't got the time to attend the meeting

This implies that you are not really interested in the meeting or that you think the meeting never achieves anything. See the next section for solutions to the latter perception.

Why have you been invited?

If you are genuinely uninterested in the meeting, consider why you have been invited. In a work situation, you are being given an opportunity to hear what is going on and have your say in how things will happen in the future. It can happen that you are invited to meetings solely because of the job that you hold. In this case, it can be useful—though courageous!—to point out that the discussion is irrelevant to you most of the time, but you want to be included when certain topics are to be discussed. Doing this can open the floodgates for a total review of what meetings are held, why, and who attends them. This can result in a more appropriate meeting framework where everyone benefits. Don't expect things to change overnight, and expect some opposition, but businesses today are much more open to constructive change.

Outside work, your experience and skills are valued by the people who run the meeting and who therefore need your input. Business and home life can put pressure on attending these meetings, but you could still consider taking a positive role by reading the papers and making your comments in writing to the Committee Secretary or the Chair.

> **PROBLEM BUSTER**
>
> Missing meetings means you are missing opportunities to make a difference. Realize that your input is important to others.

Meetings operate on the basis of compromise.

The rest of the participants never agree with my point of view

This is probably the reason why your input is valuable. If everyone at the meeting always has the same opinions and always agrees, the meeting fails to take into account other perceptions. This can mean that things are overlooked and decisions taken do not work.

Check you have understood the focus of the meeting. If you think it's about budgeting and others think it's about decision processes, you will never reach a consensus of opinion.

You should be prepared to give and take. If you don't agree with a suggestion, is it through personal prejudice or because you definitely can't see the suggestion working? Think through your reasons for disagreeing and try to have an alternative proposal. Most meetings operate on the basis of compromise.

> **PROBLEM BUSTER**
>
> Talk to the Chair. The Chair will probably tell you that your angle on the issues is important because each time the decision has been altered to take into account the facts that you have brought to the attention of the meeting.

Problems with the meeting

Nothing is decided at meetings

In the last problem of the previous section, it was stated that meetings run on the basis of compromise. However, if your meeting has a mix of participants who never agree enough to make any decision and the meeting has turned into a talking-shop, the Chair needs to take decisive action. Try some of the following solutions:

Take decisive action.

■ Attach a maximum of two proposals to each agenda item to be discussed. This means participants don't spend time thinking up a proposal and can focus on a limited range of options instead.

■ Make sure that the paperwork accompanying a meeting has as much information as possible. This cuts down lengthy background explanations at the meeting itself. The Chair can also try saying firmly to participants, 'I take it everyone has read the papers so I will take short questions on any factual queries before we move on to the discussion.'

Meetings are indispensable when you don't want to do anything.

(J. K. Galbraith, *Ambassador's Journal*, 1969)

■ To speed things up even more, contact the participants before the meeting to check that they understand the issues and to clear up any queries.

This situation can also arise when a meeting is trying to handle too big a workload. If your meeting has issues which are continually adjourned to the next meeting, then it is trying to cover too much. In this case, one of the following alternatives may be helpful:

■ *Create a sub-committee* of people who are interested in and have knowledge of the subject. Their job will be to consider all the angles, reach a maximum of two recommendations, and report back to the main meeting.

■ Have a *time limit* on the discussion. If participants know that there is only a given time to discuss a topic, they focus on the subject.

PROBLEM BUSTER

Don't let items be deferred from one meeting to the next. Allow a maximum of discussion at two meetings then make a decision—or cut the issue from the agenda.

Nothing constructive happens

This is generally down to poor follow-up by whoever puts the decisions into force. This may be for the following reasons:

■ *The decision is unworkable in practice:* If the person to carry out the decision is present at the meeting, the Chair needs to ensure that any reservations he or she has are taken into account. Sometimes, the person does not want to express this opinion when a meeting is strongly in favour of an action. The Chair needs to be alive to signals that the person is unhappy with the decision and to talk it over with them after the meeting. If necessary, the Chair needs to take the decision back to the next meeting and explain why nothing has been done.

Communicate the decision.

■ *The person implementing the decision is not sure what exactly is to be done:* Good minutes, or good communication to the person if they were not present at the meeting, should solve the second of these possibilities. A written instruction is also generally more useful than a verbal one, as the person can then keep it and refer to it when in doubt.

Use email to keep news about progress circulating to participants, especially where there is a long gap between meetings.

■ *The person implementing the decision is a poor manager:* Setting a timescale for the decision to be enacted and requiring a report on progress at the next meeting can assist with this situation. A friendly telephone call from the Chair mid-way through the timescale asking if additional assistance is needed can also be beneficial.

■ *The meeting is not being kept informed of progress:* Remember the importance of reporting back to the meeting. If the last time a meeting hears of a project is when it takes the initial decision, it can be all too easily assumed that nothing else ever happened—or ever does happen. Make it a rule that each meeting must hear something about the progress of the decisions it made at the last meeting. Even if the progress is negative, at least the meeting then has the chance to make extra suggestions for turning the situation round.

> **PROBLEM BUSTER**
>
> For a meeting to regain confidence in its powers to make things happen, try setting small, achievable goals first. Once the 'no can do' rut has been bridged, all participants will have faith in larger aims being met.

There is a general lack of interest and enthusiasm

The implication of this is that the meeting has lost its point, and is being held because it has always been held. In this case, you need to:

- Refocus on what the original **purpose of the meeting** was. Clean out the agenda and make sure that the meeting only discusses items that are connected with that original purpose.

Refocus on what the purpose of the meeting was: send all participants a list of the aims of the meeting, as well as the agenda.

So for draft 672 of this proposal we agree to drop the comma at the end of line 42?

- Hold the meeting **only when it needs to meet**: don't hold a meeting for the sake of holding a meeting. Hold it when there is something definite to discuss, and keep interest going between meetings by contacting participants to tell them of progress.

- Think of ways of **giving participants roles** so that they have an active part in the meeting and are not lookers-on. Ask them to take responsibility outside the meeting for overseeing progress on a project as well, so that they will have something they want to report on at the next meeting.

■ Impose **a time limit on discussion**. If the meeting usually lasts three hours when it could actually be held in an hour, the Chair needs to decide why it takes so long. Is someone being allowed to talk on and on? Are there too many items on the agenda? Should the meeting be split into two shorter sessions?

■ Decide if it is time to **disband this meeting** because it is no longer needed: a drastic solution but sometimes the obvious one. Sometimes the mere suggestion that the meeting should be abandoned is enough to motivate participants into looking for reasons to keep the meeting going.

PROBLEM BUSTER

A simple way to refresh a meeting that has become stagnant is to change the usual order that items are discussed in. Participants at a meeting whose topic of interest only ever comes up in the last twenty minutes will find the preceding hour very dull. Reverse the order of topics for a change every now and then.

Key participants don't turn up

Organizing and holding a meeting only to find that one or more people whose opinions are crucial do not arrive can be very frustrating both for the Chair of the meeting and for other participants. It is also a major problem for ensuring that any decision-making process operates fast enough for opportunities to be exploited, such as time-limited quotations for services and new business possibilities and, especially, press campaigns.

Meetings, are rather like cocktail parties. You don't want to go, but you're cross not to be asked.

(Jilly Cooper, *How To Survive Nine To Five*, 1970)

There are several reasons for participants' repeated non-appearance:

■ *The date or time of the meeting is not convenient:* Key participants are often the busiest members of the meeting. Check why the meeting is being held on a certain date and work with key participants to find a time which is better suited to them; even if it means sacrificing another participant.

■ *The meeting does not interest the participant:* Is this because of the previous problems discussed (nothing being decided, nothing constructive happening, lack of enthusiasm)? If you are reasonably confident that the meeting itself is not fault, consider why the participant is a key member. If they are part of the decision-making process in a work situation, talk to the person and ask if he or she is willing to delegate the decision-making. People are often ready to devolve responsibility within certain parameters if the subject does not interest them. The parameters could be budgetary (agree projects up to a certain financial limit) or other resources (agree projects which use certain contractors).

Participants should not be viewed as fixed items in meetings: change is healthy. When setting up a meeting, you may want to set a limit of two to three years' service, with an option of renewal, so that the meeting does not stagnate or become overly reliant on some participants.

PROBLEM BUSTER

Ultimately, the Chair and organizer of the meeting must decide if the participant is really key to the meeting. Look at other participants who attend regularly and show interest. Can their input be developed to take them up to 'key' level?

9 Meetings in the technological age and overseas

People can now meet around the world without leaving their desks.

Introduction

The traditional-style meeting of people sitting round a table is beginning to be replaced by a variety of new formats. The changes and advances in modern technology mean that people can now meet around the world without leaving their desks.

This chapter looks at these new types of meeting and the new rules of etiquette that they involve. Both organizers and participants should find something to interest them in this chapter, as it covers setting up a meeting and how to take part in one.

The final section discusses overseas meetings, which are still common despite the technical alternatives.

Telephone meetings

Meetings by telephone are now quite common, especially where participants live a long way apart, or even in different countries. There are several different ways of connecting people by telephone:

■ Connecting two or more people in the same building with an external caller. You can do this at home if you have two extensions by simply dialling out to the external caller on one extension, then picking up the second extension. This is a simple and cheap way to have a brief meeting without travelling. In office situations, depending on how sophisticated the telephone system is, you can connect several people in one building with one or more external callers.

■ Phone conferencing: a service provided by telephone service providers, where all callers ring a given number at a given time and are connected. Alternatively a conference coordinator from the telephone service will call each participant at a given time and connect them. The number of callers that can be connected depends on the telephone provider. Calls are charged at different rates depending on which service you choose. For example, callers can dial a free phone number so that they are not charged for the call, but the organization arranging the call will be charged.

■ Standard meeting with one participant on the phone: conference phones can be used in meetings to connect one person to the phone in the meeting room. Conference phones are specially designed to cut out background noise and to magnify voices so that both the caller and the people sitting in the room can hear clearly.

> British Telecom's website has comprehensive details of conference facilities: their address is:
>
> www.conferencing.bt.com/shocked.html
>
> Look at other telephone providers' websites such as Orange and NTL for services they can offer.

Before you hold your telephone meeting, you do need to check that this is the most appropriate way to hold your meeting. Below are a couple of examples which are suitable for phone participation:

■ single items on an agenda which need input from a participant who cannot make the face-to-face meeting: professional advisers such as solicitors and accountants are usually happy to 'attend' meetings in this way;

■ meetings involving several participants from different countries: some telephone conferencing services can also provide simultaneous translation services where more than one language is involved.

Meetings which are better not conducted by telephone include:

■ highly confidential meetings: you do need to remember that telephone calls are not always secure;

■ disciplinary meetings: reproofs should always be given face-to-face.

 Do!
ask yourself if a telephone meeting is the most appropriate method of meeting.

 Don't!
forget to check that participants are willing to take part in a telephone meeting.

You need to bear the following points in mind when holding a telephone meeting:

■ You are in a meeting. Observe the same rules as for a face-to-face meeting, for example by making sure there are no interruptions. Put yourself in a separate room if possible or, if working at home, ask your family or flatmates not to interrupt you or turn on the television next to you.

Ask your family not to interrupt you.

Make sure your voice reflects your feelings.

■ Using a good quality phone is essential. Avoid using mobile phones with background noise, or phones which are likely to cut out because the battery runs out (such as cordless phones).

■ Remember to make notes of the meeting.

■ Remember that body language is often an important part of meetings. Not being able to see that a person is smiling when they sound cross can be confusing in a phone meeting. Make sure your voice reflects your feelings.

 Do!

ask for feedback from participants on how successful they think a telephone meeting has been.

 Don't!

be afraid to experiment with the way telephone meetings are run until you find the right approach.

■ A Chair of the meeting is still vital for phone meetings, to ensure that everyone has a fair chance to speak. The Chair needs to note if someone is not talking much and, as in a face-to-face meeting, bring them into the conversation where possible.

Successful telephone meetings rely on good advance preparation. Use the following points as a guide:

■ Participants must be clearly informed of the date and time of the meeting so that they can block out the time and take steps to minimize or stop altogether any possible interruptions.

■ The same paperwork as for a normal face-to-face meeting should be circulated to all participants. If only specific items on the agenda will involve a telephone meeting, perhaps because the participant concerned with that item cannot make it to the face-to-face meeting, make it clear which these items are.

■ If this is the first time the meeting has been conducted by telephone, circulate notes to the participants explaining how the meeting will be run. You might also want to send a list of points of etiquette, as in the above list.

After your meeting, review how successful it was and if any lessons have been learnt for future telephone meetings. Keep a note of these and compare progress from one meeting to the next until you are satisfied that they work as effectively as face-to-face meetings.

Online meetings

With the growing use of home computers and more people connecting to the Internet, online meetings are a reasonably cheap and easy alternative to face-to-face meetings. An online meeting is where all participants log on to their email facility, and the discussion is held by emails containing reports, questions, replies, and suggestions being sent by one participant simultaneously to all participants (also known as an 'email broadcast'). Again, having a Chair for these meetings is important, to ensure that everyone's opinion is received and noted.

Use the growth of the Internet to connect and communicate without meeting face-to-face.

The drawback with online meetings is the delay in receiving and sending emails. Where one participant has a much slower computer, it can be very frustrating for them, as they will be permanently behind the discussion. It also needs to be remembered that not everyone has a computer: make sure you are not excluding a valuable participant if you want to arrange an online meeting.

 Do!

send attachments before the meeting if possible so time is not wasted on downloads.

 Don't!

forget that differences between Internet service providers may mean some participants experience delay in receiving emails.

The points of etiquette for online meetings are:

■ Keep your email brief and to the point.

■ Do not use abbreviations (as in text messaging) unless every-one will understand them.

■ Always have a backup phone number for participants to call so that if their computer crashes, they can notify the Chair of the meeting immediately that he or she is temporarily out of the meeting.

Keep your email brief and to the point.

■ Remember that emails are not always a secure way of send-ing information, so anything confidential should be kept to a minimum.

■ Agree whether the emails should be retained or destroyed after the meeting.

■ Remember that if several participants are connected to the same network server (for example, staff at a company), they will exchange emails more quickly between each other than with any external participants. Set a time limit for internal participants to wait before firing off the next email so that they do not inadvertently dominate the discussion.

Video conferencing is still rare but its use is increasing.

Video conferencing

Video conferencing is still relatively rare outside the commer-cial, academic, or national government worlds, but is beginning to be used more, as the work network expands across coun-tries. Some offices have their own video conferencing suites, while there are also reputable video conferencing bureaux which can provide the service. The service is not cheap, but where a face-to-face meeting would involve expensive travel, it is worthwhile doing a cost comparison to see which is the more economical alternative.

Video conferencing can involve one or more rooms being hooked up to a televising system. Participants sit before a large screen on which they can see the participants in another room. Alternatively, single video conferencing units can be attached to a computer, so that people can be connected from their desks. In this case, images of each person will appear on the computer screen. Obviously, this latter method calls for top-quality computers and a potentially large outlay on web cameras attached to each computer.

If you are involved in a video conference, take the following points into consideration:

■ There is a time lapse between a person speaking at one location and other locations receiving the signal. How long the time lapse is depends on the sophistication of the equipment. Remember to pause after each block of speech to give the other participants time to receive what you have said and take it into account in their reply.

■ Again, depending on the quality of the equipment, quick gestures and rapid movements will not transmit well. Try to keep your hands relatively still.

■ Take into account any language differences, and have a translator on standby if you are in any doubt that you might run into difficulties.

■ Most video conferences will be set up so as to have a neutral background that does not distract the viewer. However, check that any piles of paper, bags, or other items are not in full view of the camera.

 Do!

remember there may be time differences between different countries and make sure you are all using the same timetable.

 Don't!

forget to brief participants who are new to video conferencing on how the meeting works.

Overseas meetings

Plenty of meetings still involve travelling to a venue, and you may well find yourself travelling overseas at some point. The organizer has an important part in the success of an overseas meeting. Ensure that you:

■ *complete all travel arrangements:* This includes return flights, hotel bookings made and paid for, taxis or train tickets for transfers, visas, and foreign currency. A comprehensive itinerary and local map is also very useful for participants.

■ *get the timing right:* Don't book your participant on a flight that arrives less than an hour before a meeting. Flight delays, customs, and getting to the meeting itself all take time.

Travel, in the younger sort, is a part of education: in the elder, a part of experience.

(Francis Bacon, *Of Travel*)

The Foreign Office website has excellent and frequently updated advice on travelling to all countries round the world: www.fco.gov.uk

■ *check government advice on the destination country:* Your participant may need visas, vaccinations, and other items to travel safely and legally. Recent events in countries may also need to be taken into account to see if items can be imported or exported.

■ *know your participant:* Are you sure they have everything? With a disorganized participant, have a checklist right from passport to speech printout to run through with them before they leave.

As a participant, bear the following in mind when travelling:

■ A phrase book is useful for day-to-day needs, but you might also want to check up on the jargon of your own subject and jot down a list of words that are likely to crop up.

■ Check your mobile phone is activated to work in the destination country.

■ Keep all receipts, and return unused foreign currency if your organizer has arranged this for you.

■ Be sensitive to the culture of the country of your meeting: negotiating processes differ from East to West. Being alive to the local rhythms can affect the success of your meeting.

Part B: Reference section
Contents

The meeting process: a step-by-step guide

On the following two pages you will find a comprehensive flow chart of all the stages of a meeting. This is intended to provide you with a basic procedure to follow when setting up, running, and following through a meeting.

If you are not used to flow charts, the way to read them is to follow the solid arrowed lines from box to box. This gives you the basic path of all the tasks involved in the action the chart describes. An arrowed line to or from a shaded box indicates factors you need to take into consideration to do the task.

Remember, the following flow chart is only a template, and you will need to amend it according to your own meeting's requirements. Try drawing up a flow chart for your own meeting, including alternative actions if one of the steps comes to a halt. For example, if you were setting up a meeting to campaign against local building plans, your amended flow chart would show:

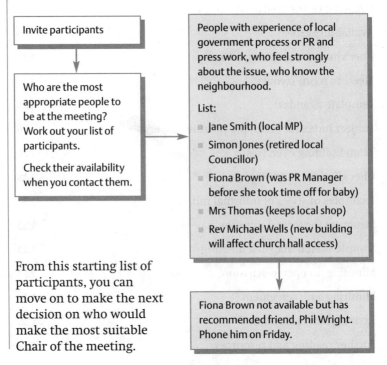

Invite participants

People with experience of local government process or PR and press work, who feel strongly about the issue, who know the neighbourhood.

Who are the most appropriate people to be at the meeting? Work out your list of participants.

Check their availability when you contact them.

List:

- Jane Smith (local MP)
- Simon Jones (retired local Councillor)
- Fiona Brown (was PR Manager before she took time off for baby)
- Mrs Thomas (keeps local shop)
- Rev Michael Wells (new building will affect church hall access)

From this starting list of participants, you can move on to make the next decision on who would make the most suitable Chair of the meeting.

Fiona Brown not available but has recommended friend, Phil Wright. Phone him on Friday.

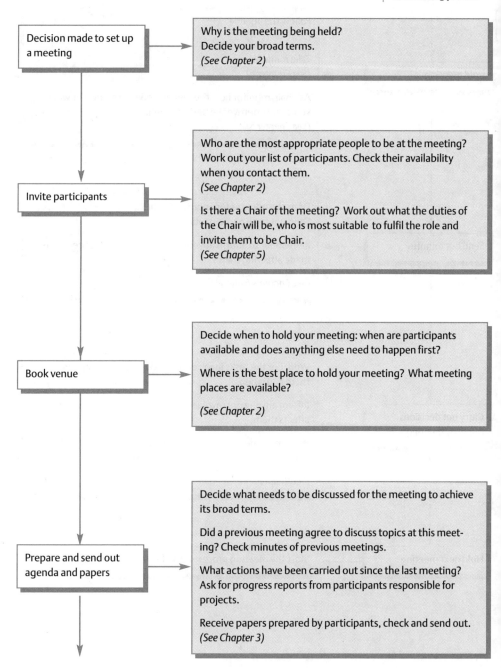

Decision made to set up a meeting
→ Why is the meeting being held?
Decide your broad terms.
(See Chapter 2)

Invite participants
→ Who are the most appropriate people to be at the meeting? Work out your list of participants. Check their availability when you contact them.
(See Chapter 2)

→ Is there a Chair of the meeting? Work out what the duties of the Chair will be, who is most suitable to fulfil the role and invite them to be Chair.
(See Chapter 5)

Book venue
→ Decide when to hold your meeting: when are participants available and does anything else need to happen first?

→ Where is the best place to hold your meeting? What meeting places are available?

(See Chapter 2)

Prepare and send out agenda and papers
→ Decide what needs to be discussed for the meeting to achieve its broad terms.

Did a previous meeting agree to discuss topics at this meeting? Check minutes of previous meetings.

→ What actions have been carried out since the last meeting? Ask for progress reports from participants responsible for projects.

Receive papers prepared by participants, check and send out.
(See Chapter 3)

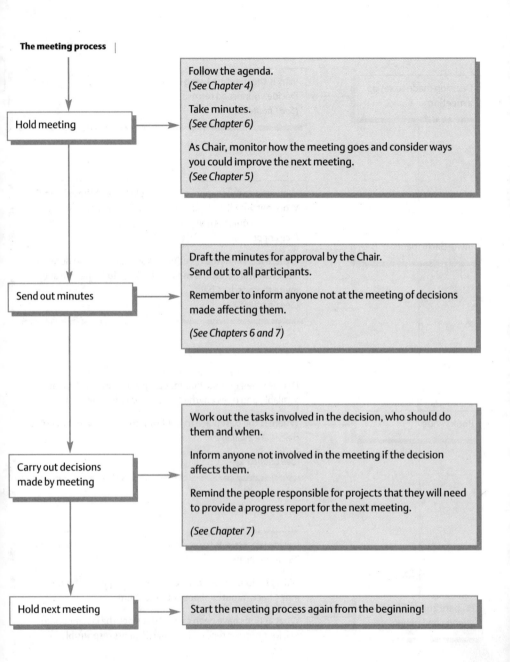

Hold meeting

Follow the agenda.
(See Chapter 4)

Take minutes.
(See Chapter 6)

As Chair, monitor how the meeting goes and consider ways you could improve the next meeting.
(See Chapter 5)

Send out minutes

Draft the minutes for approval by the Chair.
Send out to all participants.

Remember to inform anyone not at the meeting of decisions made affecting them.

(See Chapters 6 and 7)

Carry out decisions made by meeting

Work out the tasks involved in the decision, who should do them and when.

Inform anyone not involved in the meeting if the decision affects them.

Remind the people responsible for projects that they will need to provide a progress report for the next meeting.

(See Chapter 7)

Hold next meeting

Start the meeting process again from the beginning!

Checklists for organizing a meeting

Below are checklists to help you through organizing and participating in new and established meetings.

Checklist for organizing a new meeting

☐ Draw up the aims of the meeting.

☐ Make a list of potential participants.

☐ Contact potential participants and explain the purpose of the meeting to them.

☐ Contact alternative participants if need be.

☐ Agree a convenient date for the meeting.

☐ Find and book the venue (see separate checklist on pages 123–4 for organizing a venue).

☐ Draft the agenda and any accompanying papers; circulate these to participants at least one week in advance.

☐ Draft ideas on the role of the Chair (the appointment of whom and the confirmation of whose duties should be items on the agenda).

☐ Take copies of the agenda and accompanying papers to the meeting to give out in case participants forget to bring their packs.

☐ Take paper and pens for participants.

☐ Arrive at an external venue an hour in advance of the meeting and set up the room, plus any equipment that will be needed.

☐ After the meeting, write up the minutes and circulate to the participants.

☐ Carry out the decisions made by the meeting.

☐ Arrange the next meeting.

Participants' expenses

If you are able to refund any expenses incurred by participants for travelling to the meeting or for time or money spent on writing and researching reports and papers, tell participants in writing how to make their claim.

Checklist for taking over an established meeting

☐ Ask the previous organizer for training on the current way the meeting is organized; make notes about any quirks of the meeting, e.g. preferred dates, venues, equipment always needed, dietary requirements for participants.

☐ Check the timescale for sending out the agenda and accompanying papers.

☐ Contact all existing participants to introduce yourself and to agree the next meeting date, if it has not already been set.

Attendance fees

Some organizations pay participants a sum for attending the meeting. Work out a process for how payments will be made: by cheque on receipt of an invoice from the participant or through the organization's payroll if there is one.

☐ Book the venue (see separate checklist on pages 123–4 for organizing a venue).

☐ Draw up the agenda and accompanying papers or arrange for them to be written by other participants. Check the minutes of the last meeting for any agenda items which it was agreed should be included at the next meeting.

☐ Send out the agenda and papers. Collect feedback from participants on amendments to be made to the minutes of the last meeting and apologies for absence (these may be forwarded to the Minutes Secretary if there is one).

☐ Take copies of the agenda and accompanying papers to the meeting to give out in case participants forget to bring their packs.

☐ Take paper and pens for participants.

☐ Arrive at an external venue an hour in advance of the meeting and set up the room, plus any equipment that will be needed.

☐ After the meeting, write up the minutes and circulate to the participants.

☐ Carry out the decisions made by the meeting.

☐ Arrange the next meeting.

Checklist for participating in a meeting

☐ When you receive the agenda, check that all the papers which should have been included are there. If any are missing, contact the Committee Secretary or Chair.

☐ Check the date of the meeting: will you be able to attend? If so, book the time in your diary now and do not allow the appointment to be cancelled. If you cannot attend, inform the Committee Secretary or Chair.

☐ Set time aside to read through all the papers. If this is the first time you have attended this meeting, ask the Committee Secretary or Chair if you can have the minutes of the last four meetings so that you can get a feel for how the meeting works and what issues are especially important to it at the moment.

☐ As you read through the papers, make notes of any queries or comments you may have. If you do not understand any part of the papers, decide if your query should wait until the meeting or if you should contact the Chair or writer of the paper to ask for clarification.

☐ If you have attended the meeting previously and think there is an error on the minutes of the last meeting, either contact the Minutes Secretary with your suggested amendment or make a note of it to take with you to the meeting.

☐ When you attend the meeting, remember to take all the papers with you, together with notes of any queries or comments and suggestions for amendments to the minutes.

☐ You will probably need a pen and notebook to take notes or jot down questions during the meeting. A different notebook for each different type of meeting you attend is useful.

☐ If you are making a presentation, confer with the organizer of the meeting to inform them in advance of any equipment you will need such as an overhead projector or power sockets for a laptop computer and projector. Give the Minutes Secretary a hard copy of your presentation. You may also want to provide a bullet point summary to give out at the meeting to other participants.

☐ Rehearse your presentation in advance and time it: it is useful for the Chair to know how long presentations will be. If you are not sure what time you will be allowed, ask the Chair before you start writing the presentation.

☐ If, during the meeting, you agree to do something, make a note of it and after the meeting book time in your diary to do it. If you need to coordinate with others, contact them as soon as possible to arrange how and when the work is to be carried out.

☐ If you are responsible for carrying out an action, keep the meeting informed as agreed, either by a full report for the next meeting or by an interim report. If you run into difficulties with completing the project, talk to the Chair and explain.

☐ If you need to write a report or paper for the next meeting, ask the Chair or Committee Secretary when the deadline for delivery is and schedule this into your work or personal commitments.

Types of meeting

Annual General Meeting (AGM): a meeting to which all shareholders or members of a commercial company, charity, or membership society are invited. AGMs are held once a year and their purpose is to:

■ review and approve the financial accounts for the year;

■ elect members to the board;

■ discuss and vote on any constitutional or legal issues.

Extraordinary General Meeting (EGM): Sometimes an organization finds it needs to ask its shareholders or members to vote on a legal or constitutional issue midway through the year, before or after the AGM has been held. For example, if the business situation changes due to a change in the law, an organization's Memorandum and Articles may need to be updated quickly to take advantage of the new situation, rather than waiting until the AGM. In this case an EGM is held, dedicated only to the discussion of and voting on this specific issue.

Conference: Conferences are generally brainstorming sessions, attended by participants from a range of organizations,
and dedicated to one particular subject of study. Participants
will read papers on the topic and take comments and questions
from other participants. For example, academic conferences
will consider a subject such as discoveries in a branch of
physics; the conference offers the opportunity to share these
discoveries with others studying the same subject.

At industry or trade association conferences, there is often a
final summing-up session when the conference will make broad
recommendations for the member organizations to follow. In
government, they are often known as **summit meetings**.

Board meeting: a meeting of the directors or governors of an
organization. Generally held several times a year, the meeting
takes place to cover a range of strategic issues which affect the
organization as a whole. These could include:

- the financial situation of the organization: budgeting,
  reviewing, agreeing a major expenditure;

- reviewing the policies of the company;

- deciding on new projects and lines of business;

- reviewing progress on ongoing projects;

- deciding on property matters such as office moves or property purchases;

- employment issues: setting salary levels, reviewing senior
  staff's performance, proposals to unions recognized in the
  organization, staff pensions.

Management meeting: a meeting of the managers who carry
out the day-to-day running of the organization. Topics could
include :

- determining how to put into practice decisions taken by the
  board meeting;

- deciding on proposals to put to the Board;

- progress reviews on ongoing projects;

- decisions that do not require approval by the Board (such as
  internal promotions, newsletters);

■ communications with other organizations, staff, and the press;

■ preparing for other meetings.

All the above are examples of main meetings. The following types of meeting are set up by the main meeting.

Sub-committee meeting: sub-committees may be set up by board or management meetings to discuss and review a single topic or to manage a given project. Sub-committees have limited powers of decision-making, and report back to the meeting which set them up. Generally, the topics require the discussion of complex information—too long to be considered properly at the main meeting which sets it up. Appropriate topics are:

■ Design issues: logos, stationery. The sub-committee may talk to outside design companies and recommend to the main meeting which company the organization should use.

■ Staff issues: A staff benefits sub-committee might review the market for an appropriate pension provider. Sub-committees may also be formed to provide a 'bridge' between directors, managers, and junior staff, where ideas can be discussed and news from all sides of the organization shared.

■ Financial matters: an organization's budget is often drawn up by a sub-committee and presented by one of the committee to the main meeting. The budget sub-committee will meet at regular intervals through the year to check that the company is on track for both income and expenditure.

Branch meeting: Trade unions and national membership societies such as the National Trust will usually have branch organizations to give feedback to the main body. Branches may have certain powers to organize matters in their own area. Their meetings are centred round:

■ local issues: local projects, membership in the neighbourhood, local fundraising and awareness campaigns;

■ the relationship between the branch and the national body;

■ reporting back local feelings and suggestions for both local and national projects to the main organization;

■ local social events held by the branch.

Standing committee: A standing committee is set up by a main meeting to discuss and/or manage a topic. Unlike a sub-committee, which usually has a limited life-span, standing committees are permanent features of an organization. Standing committees may discuss:

- staff issues: standing committees may be the appropriate place for disciplinary issues to be resolved;

- fundraising: the standing committee may be in charge of organizing a particular event, perhaps the annual ball.

Steering committee: A steering committee is a discussion forum concentrating on one topic. The committee will make recommendations on actions or policies to the main meeting. Steering committees are usually permanent features, but should only meet when there is a need for them to discuss their particular topic. Issues that steering committees discuss could include:

- ethical issues: green policies for manufacturing industries, opening up the services of the business to customers with physical or mental impairments;

- business development: determining if a potential new area of business 'fits' the existing company's portfolio of services.

Any of the above meetings, main or subsidiary, may be encountered in any type of organization from commerce to membership societies. Where an office is involved, the following meetings may also take place:

- **appraisals**: meetings to review and discuss individual performance;

- **staff meetings**: meetings to put forward staff views to management or vice versa;

- **departmental meetings**: meetings to discuss and manage the work of a department;

- **team meetings**: meetings to discuss and manage the work of a team.

You will find other titles given to meetings, as each organization tends to have its own names for them, but most meetings fit into one of the above categories.

Is the name of your meeting appropriate?

Sometimes any work that participants do in a meeting can be hampered by the fact that the name of their meeting carries negative connotations for people outside the meeting. For example, if for years an organization has a steering committee on business development which is seen as being slow to reach decisions or which rarely approves suggestions from staff or members, it may be time to start again from scratch, rethinking the aims and how the meeting works. Don't, however, change the name merely to reflect a passing fashion: there needs to be a genuine change in the way the meeting works and, perhaps, its participants.

Communications between meetings

Communications between meetings

When writing a report for a different meeting, make sure you use that meeting's style and terminology so that there is no confusion.

Good communication between main and offshoot meetings is the key to their success. When you set up a sub-meeting of any sort, make sure there is a practical and efficient form of communication between the two and that it is clear who's in charge of this process. Below is an example of a flow chart showing how the communication process between a staff meeting and the board meeting works in practice.

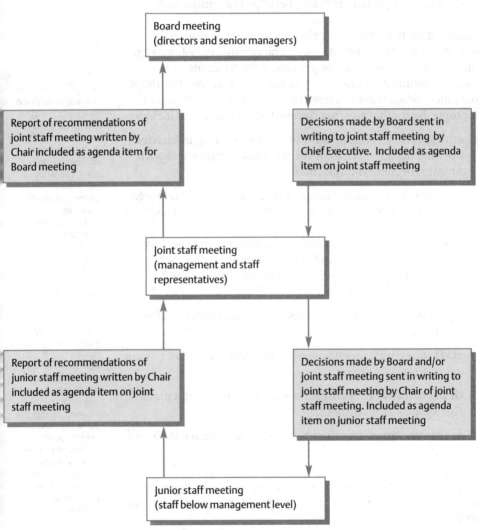

Board meeting
(directors and senior managers)

Report of recommendations of joint staff meeting written by Chair included as agenda item for Board meeting

Decisions made by Board sent in writing to joint staff meeting by Chief Executive. Included as agenda item on joint staff meeting

Joint staff meeting
(management and staff representatives)

Report of recommendations of junior staff meeting written by Chair included as agenda item on joint staff meeting

Decisions made by Board and/or joint staff meeting sent in writing to joint staff meeting by Chair of joint staff meeting. Included as agenda item on junior staff meeting

Junior staff meeting
(staff below management level)

Latin phrases used at meetings

cf. short for the Latin 'confer', which in this context has a slightly different meaning to the English 'confer'. It here means 'compare'.

Example: cf. the proposal made by the Finance Committee not to sanction further expenditure in this area.

i.e. a generally used abbreviation of the Latin 'id est' for 'that is'.

Example: if you write a report from one meeting for another meeting, use the latter's terminology, i.e. don't use 'Chair' if the meeting calls its leader a 'Chairman'.

in absentia literally 'in the absence of'. Used when someone is not present at a meeting.

Example: It was noted and accepted that the company seal was fixed to the lease, in absentia the Chief Executive who was on holiday

nem con short for 'nemine contradicente', which means 'no-one speaking against'. Used during voting at a meeting: a vote passed 'nem con' means no-one voted against the proposal.

Example: The proposal was agreed, nem con.

status quo meaning 'the current situation'. Usually heard in phrases like 'keeping the status quo' or 'maintaining the status quo', meaning that no change will be made to things as they stand.

Example: The meeting decided the status quo in respect of income was acceptable.

stet meaning 'let it stand'. Used when editing documents by hand where a sentence or paragraph has been crossed out in error—the 'stet' cancels the crossing out.

Example: The ~~Chair stated~~ that the next meeting would be on 15th December. *stet*

115

Do!

take the time to learn about financial terms and how to read accounts: ask the organization if they can provide training, or consider buying for yourself a couple of guides.

Don't!

rely on other participants' accounting knowledge: make sure you are satisfied.

Financial terms used at meetings

If you are involved in a meeting which looks at the organization's accounts, it is very important to understand what you are being asked to review. Below are a few of the terms you may encounter. Think about building up your own list for reference in the future.

■ **Accounting period:** the time covered by a set of accounts. All organizations will at least produce annual accounts but most will issue accounts several times a year for directors to inspect to check the financial health of the organization. Internal accounts for managers to check their own department's spending and income may be issued every month.

■ **Accrual:** an adjustment made to the accounts to allow for an expenditure for which no invoice has yet been received but which will have to be paid before the next accounting period.

■ **Asset:** anything which has a value which is owned by the organization. These assets may be **fixed** or **tangible** (such as money in the bank, property, equipment) or **intangible** (such as customer goodwill or a patent). A **liquid asset** is one that can be sold, reasonably quickly, to raise money (such as furniture or computer equipment).

■ **Audit:** an authorized check made of an organization's accounts, usually carried out at the end of each financial year, by the **auditors**, who are chartered accountants.

■ **Budget:** a forecast of what income will be received over a given period (usually a year) and what expenditure will be incurred. An organization **sets a budget** to plan its financial management for the year, calculating what it can afford to spend (on staff, new equipment, rent) and what profit it will make from the income it will receive.

When studying accounts, you need to remember that they are always slightly out of date purely because of the time it takes to assemble them.

■ **Company** or **management accounts:** The accounts presented to a meeting usually consist of at least three statements:

○ **the balance sheet:** a snapshot of the financial value of all assets owned by the company at a given date, together with all outstanding bills;

- the **cash flow statement:** shows what money has been paid out and what paid in during a period;

- the **profit and loss account:** an explanation of invoices issued and received during the period.

Financial terms used at meetings

Company accounts may also show the actual expenditure and income versus the budgeted expenditure and income. This is an important sheet, and you should keep an eye out for any large variations between the two sets of figures. A well-presented set of accounts will include explanatory notes: check these for the explanation between the figures, and if they are not clear, ask at the meeting for further clarification.

■ **Corporation Tax:** All companies are liable to pay Corporation Tax. The amount of tax is set by the government, and the amount due per company is determined by the **taxable income** of the company. Companies with a turnover over a set amount must also register for **value added tax (VAT)** and charge VAT on their services.

For more information on tax issues, check the Inland Revenue's website, www.inlandrevenue. gov.uk

■ **Debenture:** a type of loan taken out by a commercial company from an external third party, who will receive shares or money in exchange.

■ **Depreciation:** Just as, when you own a car, its value decreases over time, so the value of an organization's fixed assets (computers, furniture, etc.) decreases over the years. Accountants take this fall in value into account through the process of *depreciation*, and lower the value of the assets in the balance statement. Accounting practice sets the percentage rate at which the value of an asset decreases each year.

If you participate in the meetings of a company which has assets such as property which it owns outright or works of art, these assets may, conversely, **appreciate** in value over the years, i.e. increase.

Amortization is the term applied to the decreasing value of intangible assets such as a brand name or a software licence.

■ **Dividend:** the money paid to a shareholder from the profits a company makes in a year. The amount of the dividend depends on the amount of the profit available for distribution to shareholders, and the number of shares an individual holds.

■ **Exceptional item:** an expense incurred by the company in the course of its usual business but which is much larger than usual, For example, if the company has a normal budget of £15,000 for legal expenses but in the period covered by the accounts spends £45,000 because of a court case, the accounts should carry an explanation of the reason for this steep rise.

■ **Extraordinary item:** an item on the account which either was not budgeted for or is very unlikely to appear again regularly in the accounts. Examples are redundancy payments to staff or the purchase of a piece of equipment.

■ **Ledgers:** Most organizations have three 'ledgers' to record all their financial transactions. The term dates from the time when accounts were handwritten in ledgers. Most companies now rely on computer spreadsheets or accounting programs, but they retain the term.

The **purchase ledger** records the individual amounts of purchases made by the organization, and from which companies and individuals.

The **sales ledger** logs all the invoices issued and customers to which the organization sells anything.

The **nominal ledger** shows all the items included on a company's accounts. Every individual or company who invoices the organization or is invoiced by it is set up in this system as a **nominal account**.

■ **Liability:** a debt owed by the company to another party. A **contingent liability** is an expense that has not yet been confirmed: it may or may not be incurred, such as the possible purchase of a piece of equipment to replace one that is faulty.

■ **Market value:** the price an external third party would be willing to pay for an asset owned by the organization. **Open market value** is an extension of this term when the asset would be available to anyone interested.

■ **Net book value:** the value of an asset as it is logged in the company's registers, after allowing for depreciation.

- **Offsetting:** an organization may reduce its tax liabilities by claiming costs for purchases, development, and training. This process is known as offsetting.

- **Overheads:** the charges an organization incurs which are not directly connected to the services it provides. Usually these charges relate to the property or offices it occupies. Rent, rates, service charges, heating, and lighting all come into this category.

- **Trade creditors:** These are individuals or companies who are owed money by the organization. They may also be referred to as **accounts payable**.

  Trade debtors or **accounts receivable** are those individuals or companies who owe the organization money.

- **Turnover:** the actual amount of money received by a company during the accounting period. This is not quite the same as the profit of a company. The amount of expenditure is deducted from the turnover amount to provide the amount of profit.

- **Write off:** assets which would no longer fetch more than a fraction of their original purchase price are 'written off' in the accounts and removed from the list of assets.

Availability table

Chapter 2 discussed how to fix a date for a meeting by checking when participants were available. When contacting participants, tabling out their names against a list of dates can help.

A blank table is shown below. The participants' names are down the left side and possible dates in the remaining rows.

	15th	16th	17th	18th
John				
Sue				
Chris				
Clare				

Financial terms used at meetings

Insurance policies

Prudent companies will insure themselves against unforeseen disasters. All companies should have **public liability insurance** so that if a visitor to the company has an accident this policy will pay any claim made by them. **Employers' liability insurance** pays out on employees' claims for injury or illness caused at work. **Directors' and officers' insurance** covers any claim made against the directors or senior managers of a company for negligence or other forms of mismanagement. If you are classed as a director, you might want to check that your company has adequate insurance in this last category.

Availability table

	15th	16th	17th	18th
John	all day	no	all day	a.m. only
Sue		couldn't contact		
Chris	no	all day	all day	all day
Clare	all day	a.m. only	all day	no

Use an email to find a date for a meeting convenient to all participants.

The completed table. Sue could not be contacted, so no dates are filled in. Clare and John can only make the morning of some days. The 17th is the day that all contacted participants can manage, so the date can be fixed.

An alternative method to find a date if all participants have email is to send out an email with suggested dates, asking participants to write their name against the dates when they could attend and then simply send the email back to you. For example:

Dear All

The next sub-committee meeting is due to be held in May. Please sign against the dates given below on which you would be able to attend a meeting:

■ Tuesday 10th May

■ Thursday 17th May

■ Friday 18th May

Please reply by 1st May.

Kind regards

Helen

Checklist for organizing a venue

Organizing the venue for a meeting involves a number of issues. Use the checklist below to make sure that you cover all eventualities.

☐ Decide what sort of venue will best suit your meeting. A formal meeting needs a formal setting, an informal discussion somewhere that will encourage a relaxed atmosphere.

☐ If you have access to meeting rooms at an office, check with whoever is in charge of booking rooms if the room you want is free, and book it as soon as possible.

☐ If you are looking for an external venue, draw up a shortlist of possible places. Find venues through the recommendation of other participants, previous use, using a professional venue finder, searching local directories, or the Internet.

☐ Contact the conference manager of external venues, and book an appointment to look at the facilities and discuss the meeting's requirements.

☐ Make a list of what the meeting needs including

○ the number of participants;

○ how the room is to be laid out;

○ refreshments required (anything from coffee and biscuits to a three-course meal);

○ equipment needed: overhead projectors, flipcharts, projector screen, lectern, telephones, power sockets for laptop computers and projectors, a table for literature to be displayed, induction loop for the hard of hearing, PA equipment, video and television;

○ any facilities required for participants with a physical impairment, such as wheelchair access.

Remember to take this list with you when you visit the venue.

☐ At your meeting with the conference manager, confirm the prices of everything and whether or not these include VAT.

☐ If you are arranging a series of meetings, ask if the venue can offer a discount for advance and multiple bookings.

☐ When you have finished inspecting all venues, make your final decision and confirm all the details in writing to the conference manager.

☐ Some venues may require a deposit in advance; make sure that this is paid promptly to avoid losing the booking.

☐ If you have a lot of equipment that needs to be taken to the venue, decide what is the best way for it to be taken there. Professional conference organizers will collect, set up, dismantle and return items such as exhibition stands and furniture. Usually the quickest and cheapest option is a taxi. Ask the conference manager when you can have access to the room to set up the equipment.

☐ A couple of days before the meeting, check that everything is all right with the venue and assemble all the equipment that will be needed. If you need assistance to set up the room, organize your volunteers.

☐ On the day of the meeting, arrive an hour in advance to set up the room and to greet participants. Make contact with the conference manager at the venue so that he or she knows where to find you if need be.

Meeting room layouts

When booking a room, you will be asked if you want the room laid out in 'boardroom' or 'conference' style.

Boardroom style is suitable for most meetings which involve sitting round a table.

Conference or theatre style is suitable for AGMs, EGMs, and other meetings which involve a form of presentation or question-and-answer session in front of an audience.

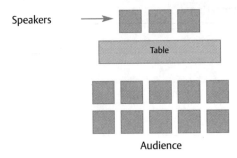

A less formal layout is more appropriate for informal meetings. Consider dispensing altogether with a table and sitting 'in the round'. However, please remember the Minutes Secretary if you use this arrangement, and provide some form of writing surface for him or her.

A popular form of current office layout is to have what is called a 'teardrop' end to a standard desk round which two or three chairs can be placed, providing a meeting area.

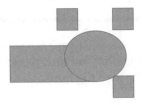

Tip
Sitting behind a desk for an 'informal chat' can be counter-productive as the desk forms a barrier. Move away from the desk to a round meeting table, or place seats in the centre of the room.

See Chapter 3.

Template agendas

Agendas for formal meetings should be written on the organization's notepaper. When an agenda is combined with an invitation to a meeting, the name of the company or Committee Secretary should be included at the bottom.

Below is an example of a formal agenda.

You are invited to a meeting of the school governors of St Dominic's, to be held at 4pm on Tuesday, 16th March 2001 in the school library.

Agenda

1. Adoption of agenda

2. Apologies for absence

3. Minutes of the last meeting

4. Matters arising

5. Finance

    5.1 accounts to 28th February 2001 (attached)

    5.2 fundraising reports (attached)

    5.3 appointment of new Treasurer

6. School inspection report (attached)

7. After school club (report to be tabled)

8. Date of next meeting

9. Any other business

James Gill
Headmaster

This agenda clearly shows what papers have been included for reading prior to the meeting and those which will be available for the first time at the meeting itself.

The agenda of an AGM, printed on the company's letterhead, would be similar to the following:

You are invited to attend the seventh Annual General Meeting of the Liverpool & District Parks & Gardens Society Ltd, to be held at 7pm on Tuesday 23rd May 2001, at the Old Meeting House, 47 Westway Street, Birkenhead, Merseyside L51 2VB.

Agenda

1. Apologies for absence

2. Minutes of the last meeting

3. Election of board members.
   Following the retirement of Mrs Thelma Farrell, a vacancy has arisen.
   The following nomination has been received: Mrs Sarah Myers.

4. To receive the accounts for the year ending 31st April 2001

5. To appoint Adam Brown & Sons as auditors for the company

6. Any other business

BY ORDER OF THE COMPANY SECRETARY

Mark Westfield

Mark Westfield

For informal or internal meetings, a memo such as the one given below on plain paper will be fine.

Memo
From: Sarah Smith
To: All members of the staff newsletter editorial committee
Date: 15th May 2001

Re: **Next meeting—29th May 2001**

We agreed last time that we should discuss
- looking for a new printing company
- articles for the next edition.

If anyone else has anything else to add to this list, could you let me know by the end of the week.

An email is ideal for this type of informal agenda.

Subject index for archiving meeting papers

See Chapter 3 under 'Keeping track of your paperwork'.

For most meetings papers, the following subject headings would be standard:

- **Finance:** reports on accounts, fundraising, costs, agreements to spend money, banking arrangements;

- **Constitutional matters:** reports and proposals on how the organization and the meeting operates;

- **Participants:** elections to the meeting, resignations, appointment of observers, election of Chair and other officers;

- **Minutes:** copies of past minutes;

- **Action points:** filed separately, so that you can see at a glance what should have happened when.

Create sections in your file for each specific topic or project that the meeting discusses.

Note that papers may need to be filed under more than one section if they relate to a variety of subjects. In this case, either:

- photocopy the paper and file copies in each subject section (though this will add to the bulk of your filing system);

- put the paper in the section of your file to which most of the paper refers and add notes in the additional sections stating where the paper is;

- if you have an electronic copy of the paper, cut and paste the paragraphs which relate to different subjects into separate documents.

Team-building exercises

Introducing participants to each other

See Chapter 5.

At a newly convened meeting, ask the participants to pair up (or divide into twos and threes if they are an unequal number of participants) and spend five minutes talking to each other. At the end of the five minutes, participants introduce their partners to the rest of the meeting, giving their name, occupation, and why they are at the meeting.

This is a good ice-breaker as participants immediately get to know at least one other person at the meeting. It also gives all participants some knowledge of the background of their fellow meeting members and therefore an idea of the issues which will be important to them.

Keeping participants on track

Ask participants to state what they think the five aims of the meeting are.

This is an exercise for established meetings with participants who are comfortable talking in front of each other. It is useful for meetings which are beginning to be vague about their purpose and is best done without prior warning, at the start of the meeting, before the agenda is taken. This reminder of what the participants are there to do can help the subsequent discussions.

Restoring confidence

At the end of the meeting, ask all participants to name one *positive* feeling they have about that day's meeting.

This is an exercise needing careful handling, but is useful to restore the confidence of a meeting which has had tough issues and decisions to make, or has not been able to move its business further forward for some time. Even if participants only come up with the comment 'the coffee was good', at least this raises a laugh and means participants leave on a more positive note.

Checklists for minuting

Preparing to take minutes

Have you got all the following?

☐ a list of the participants;

☐ a copy of the agenda and all accompanying papers;

☐ a copy of any formal resolutions being proposed;

☐ a copy of any presentations being given;

☐ a notebook and at least two pens;

☐ a clipboard to balance your notebook on if there is no table;

☐ a copy of the minutes of the last meeting for signature;

☐ another copy of the minutes of the last meeting to write amendments on;

☐ copies of any already received suggested amendments to the minutes;

☐ notes of apologies for absence from any participants;

☐ a diary and a list of dates for future meetings.

And ...

☐ Have you checked for any in camera sessions or changes of Chair during the meeting?

Writing up minutes

Use the following guidelines to help you write up minutes:

☐ Write up minutes no more than a week after the meeting takes place.

☐ Decide on the style of your minutes and draw up a blank template with all the headings.

☐ Fill in one section at a time.

☐ Keep a list of all the abbreviations and acronyms you use and make a glossary of these at the end of your document.

☐ Make an action point list, noting down all the things that the meeting agreed were to be done, who is to do them, and any deadlines agreed.

☐ Make a note of all the items the meeting agreed to discuss at the next meeting, and pass this on to the Chair or Committee Secretary for them to include on the next agenda. Remember to add page numbers.

☐ If using a word-processor, save your document at the end of each section.

☐ Do not start new topics or put headings at the bottom of a page.

☐ If using a word processor, in your completed minutes hide the borders from any tables you use to write your text in, as these can be distracting for the reader.

☐ Put your minutes on one side for a time when you complete them, and then reread them for errors. If word-processing, print out the document and check the hard copy for mistakes.

☐ Circulate the minutes to the Chair and other appropriate participants for their comments. Give them a deadline to send amendments to you by.

☐ Wait until you receive feedback from everyone before making changes.

If word-processing minutes, on the bottom of the last page put the name of the document you save your minutes in so that you can find it again easily. You may also want to add the date and a draft number so that you know which version you are working on. For example 'Janboardminutes/ ver 2'.

Examples of styles of informal minutes

All informal minutes should start with the date of the meeting and a list of who was present.

17th January 2001: Management meeting

Present: Neil Green (NG), Hayley Thomas (HT), Peter Smith (PS), Rav Barsati (RB), Julie George (JG)

Bullet point minutes

The easiest style of minutes. Each decision or report in progress is condensed into one or two sentences.

■ HT reported advert for new administrator would be included in the newspaper on Tuesday.

■ RB said that the training programme for new staff had been delayed due to the illness of the Training Manager.

■ NG reminded HT to obtain quotes for new computers for new staff.

Rolling minutes

In this style, minutes are laid out in a table with reference to past minutes and a space for future actions. These are useful for keeping track of what's happening in project situations or when there are many tasks on the go.

Subject	Person in charge	Progress	Action
Budget	Neil	Draft budgets received from IT, Personnel and Sales. Awaiting budgets from Training and Customer Service.	RB to chase Training. HT to chase Customer Service Budgets to be in by 25th Jan.

At the next meeting, your minutes might be written up as follows:

Subject	Person in charge	Progress	Action
Budget	Hayley (prev. Neil)	All draft budgets now received. NG has amalgamated onto one spreadsheet	HT to convene meeting of Finance sub-comm. Meeting in early Feb to give full draft budget to Board at end of Feb.

This clearly shows the change of the responsible person and the deadlines which now need to be met.

Narrative style

Useful for reporting on small meetings (three to six people), especially appraisals and other personnel issues.

JG said that she had benefited from the external training arranged by HT, but was disappointed that she had not been able to have the planned weekly meeting with PS. PS agreed that these meetings had not worked out, because he had been working out of the office over the last three months. It was agreed that where PS was unable to make the meeting, HT would stand in for him, and a report would be emailed to PS after each meeting.

Structure for formal minutes

See Chapter 7.

Laying out a blank template and then filling in the gaps can help you structure your minutes. It's also easier to write minutes when they are broken down into small sections, as you can focus on the specific section. Also useful if you are likely to be interrupted—you can finish small sections quickly and not lose the thread of your line of thought.

Below is an example of a template, with sections starting to be completed.

Private and Confidential

Minutes of a meeting of the Fundraising Committee, held on 20th January 2001, at Wiston Village Hall.

Present: Gina Bridges (Chair)
Mark Helmsley
Kate Jones
Elaine Samson
Clive Thomas (Minutes Secretary)

In Attendance: Paula Cooper (Accountant)

1. Adoption of the agenda

2. Apologies for absence

3. Finance

3.1 Accounts to 31st December 2000

3.2 Donations

4. Proposed 'celebrity' auction

5. New charity legislation on fundraising

6. Date of next meeting

7. Any other business

Sample sketch map of a meeting

When you attend a meeting for the first time, whether as Minutes Secretary or a participant, it can be helpful to make a quick sketch map to fix names to faces.

See Chapter 6.

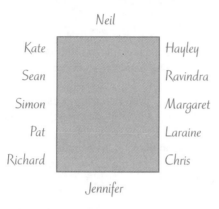

Minuting an open discussion

As an example, suppose that an action group is discussing ways to make their campaign known. Your notes read as follows.

See Chapter 6.

Simon: Write to the local MP.

Laraine: Get article in local newspaper.

Chris: Agrees with Simon and thinks should also get posters in local shops.

Pat: Knows someone at local newspaper: will contact them.

Richard: Need more people in the area to know about the campaign.

Kate: Thinks writing to local MP waste of time at this stage; need to get local feeling raised and momentum going so have weight of local opinion to get MP interested.

Sean: Agrees: concentrate on local people first.

Ravindra: Agrees with Chris about posters in local shops: can produce these on his computer.

Margaret: Also make flyers to hand out to people: shops can have bundles of these for people to pick up.

Rather than giving each person's comment, in the written-up minutes group comments of a similar nature together so that the minutes read more logically. Following this rule, the written-up minutes of the discussion given above would read as follows:

Raising Awareness

The meeting then discussed how to bring the campaign to public notice and the following points were made:

■ running a poster and flyer campaign in the local shops. Ravindra Barsati kindly offered to produce the posters and flyers.

■ getting an article in the local newspaper. Pat Hannon will contact her friend at the paper to see how this can be achieved

■ writing a letter to the local MP. The meeting generally felt that this should be done after local awareness of the campaign has been raised and there is sufficient support for the letter to the MP to carry weight.

If you are minuting a meeting where participants prefer to be credited for their suggestions, you would need to expand these minutes slightly so that they would read as follows:

■ Chris Miles, Ravindra Barsati and Margaret Williams suggested running a poster and flyer campaign in the local shops. Ravindra Barsati kindly offered to produce the posters and flyers.

■ Laraine Peters and Pat Hannon proposed getting an article in the local newspaper. Pat Hannon will contact her friend at the paper to see how this can be achieved

■ Simon Barnard and Chris Miles were in favour of writing a letter to the local MP. Kate Hansford and Sean Thomas were not in favour of this suggestion, and after further discussion, the meeting agreed that this should be done after local awareness of the campaign has been raised. There would then be sufficient support for the letter to the MP to carry weight.

Tip
Read through copies of past minutes if available to see if suggestions must be credited to individual participants or if general anonymous minutes of comments are acceptable. Suggestions for improving company performance or business turnover and strong disagreements with a proposed policy change should usually be individually credited.

Minuting a disagreement

Learning how to note and write up minutes of a disagreement calls for a good deal of tact on the part of the Minutes Secretary. Check past minutes to see how previous disagreements have been handled. If this is a new meeting, talk to the Chair about how much detail of the disagreement should be included.

See Chapter 6.

As an example, suppose the local campaign group had an argument about whether or not to invite the local MP to their launch party.

Your notes might read as follows:

Sean: Mentioned to the MP that he might like to give the opening speech at launch party.

Simon: No way! MP did not reply to the first two letters sent and has only started being involved now because of local opinion.

Kate: Agrees with Simon, but having the MP would give the party weight and would attract reporters—get coverage for campaign.

Margaret: MP should not be invited: thinks that MP does not really support the campaign.

Laraine: Why did Sean mention this to MP without asking the rest of the meeting?

Sean: When he met MP, mentioned launch party and MP said he would like to come.

Laraine: He can come, but not to give speech! Sean should not have asked him.

Richard: This is second time Sean has done something without referring to the meeting.

Sean: Sorry, but it was a good opportunity.

Chris: Sean must refer to the meeting on important points like this.

The written-up minutes of this dicussion would read as follows:

Launch Party

The meeting was concerned that Sean Thomas had mentioned to the local MP that he might be invited to give the opening speech at the launch party. The meeting stressed that Sean Thomas must refer all such matters to them in future before taking action.

There was general agreement that the MP was welcome to the party but not to give the speech, in view of the MP's ambivalent attitude to the campaign. However, if the MP confirmed he was coming, the press should be informed he was on the guest list.

Action point templates

See Chapter 7.

To help participants remember and plan what they need to do after a meeting, a précis or action point list of the decisions taken is very useful. This list can also be circulated to other people not present at the meeting who do not need to know all the discussions which took place at the meeting but do need to know what implications they have for them.

You could lay out your list in a table as follows:

	Action point	Who	When
1.	New sub-committee to discuss design of new school sports hall	Kate (organizer), Philip, Jean, Aaron	Meet in next 2 weeks: report next meeting

Outstanding action point template

This is an extension of the first action point list, and lets meeting participants see at a glance what progress is being made on decisions made at previous meetings.

Date of meeting	Action point	To do
20th Jan 2001	Set up new sub-committee to discuss design of new school sports hall	Report to main meeting

Report must be in at next meeting |

Further reading and resources

This last section provides you with ideas on developing your meeting skills.

Further reading

Books on business and management skills tend to fall into two categories: the short, which concentrate on practical issues and general advice, and the long, which concentrate on a specific area and the theories behind it. Buying a mixture of both categories of books is important.

Books for all

See the list at the beginning of this book for other titles in the One Step Ahead series which cover in more depth subjects which have been briefly covered in this book.

Other series include:

- The *Institute of Personnel Development* (website address: www.ipd.co.uk) has a series of short books on various aspects of team building, management and administration that are accessible and practical.

- The Institute of Management's *Successful in a Week* series, published by Hodder & Stoughton.

- *Business Action Pocketbooks* published by Thorogood.

- The *Business Basics* series published by How To Books.

- The *Dummies* and *Complete Idiot's Guides* are two light-hearted series which cover a good range of topics. Bear in mind that they are for an American audience.

 Do!

'try before you buy' by borrowing expensive books from your local public library.

 Don't!

forget to ask colleagues and friends for recommendations.

Reading for Chairs and Committee Secretaries

■ *The Institute of Directors* with Kogan Page publishes directors' guides (website address: www.iod.co.uk) suitable for both new and experienced board directors.

■ *Chairing The Board: A Practical Guide to Activities and Responsibilities*, John Harper, Kogan Page.

■ *Running Board Meetings*, Patrick Dunne, Kogan Page.

■ *Essential Manager's Manual*, Robert Heller and Tim Hindle, Dorling Kindersley.

Specific skills

Meetings

■ *The ICSA Meetings and Minutes Handbook*, A. Hamer, ICSA Publishing.

■ *Encyclopaedia of Corporate Meetings, Minutes and Resolutions*, edited by William Sardell, Prentice-Hall.

■ *Meetings that Work*, Catherine Widdicombe, Lutterworth Press.

Report writing

■ *How To Write Effective Reports*, John Sussams, Gower Publishing.

■ *Professional Report Writing*, Simon Mort, Gower Publishing.

Presenting

■ *Successful Presentation Skills*. Andrew Bradbury, Kogan Page.

■ *Effective Presentation*, Ros Jay, Financial Times, Prentice Hall.

■ *The Oxford Guide to Writing and Speaking*, John Seely, Oxford University Press.

Minutes

■ *Taking Minutes of Meetings*, Joanna Gutmann, Kogan Page.

Reading financial accounts

■ *Accounts Demystified*, Anthony Rice, Prentice-Hall.

Team-building exercises

■ *The Big Book of Business Games: Icebreakers, Creativity Exercises and Meeting Energizers*, John Newstrom and Edward Scannell, McGraw-Hill Training Series.

Websites

The explosion in the use of the Internet means that there is a wealth of knowledge available at the press of a button. To save you time searching for the right website, below are some of the more useful websites. If you use these as starting points, look out for links on these to other subjects.

Language and writing

AskOxford www.AskOxford.com. A fun and informative site about the English language.

The Plain English Campaign www.plainenglish.co.uk. A site giving advice on writing without jargon and intelligibly for any audience. Includes guides on writing and on financial, legal, and medical terms.

Professional associations

The Institute of Management Foundation www.inst-mgt.org.uk. The Institute's mission is to promote 'the art and science of management'. Its Management Information Centre, available to members, holds a huge array of articles on management, many available online.

Tip
Local debating societies can also help you. Attending a few meetings of the society, whether you take an active part or just listen, will give you ideas about how to present an argument, respond to opinions, and discuss topics.

Further reading and resources

The Industrial Society www.indsoc.co.uk. The Industrial Society promotes good working practices in commercial and non-commercial organizations. Its website has details of courses and publications, on aspects of meetings and the skills they require.

Information on agenda items

Directors' Briefings at www.bizhot.co.uk has over 150 short four-page guides on topics including law, finance, information technology, and tax.

Learning online

There are a growing number of companies such as Easycando (www.easycando.com) which offer online courses. World Wide Learn (www.worldwidelearn.com) offers lists of training courses available online.

Acknowledgements

Many thanks to the following people who willingly gave their time and assistance: John Seely, series editor, for suggesting this book and his advice in its writing; Alysoun Owen and Helen Cox of OUP for their patience and guidance; Jonathan Woods for advice on financial terminology; Russell Smith for suggesting several best practice examples; Gill Ellis, Jackie Luke and Jane Chamberlain for sharing experiences of non-work-based and other types of meetings.

I am indebted as well to the Chairs, Directors, Company Secretaries, Legal Advisers and other meeting participants with whom it is and has been my pleasure to work.

Index